A CALL TO ACTION:

Practically Reversing the Trends of Mass Incarceration

By

Dr. Herron Keyon Gaston

RoseDog Books

PITTSBURGH, PENNSYLVANIA 15238

The contents of this work including, but not limited to, the accuracy of events, people, and places depicted; opinions expressed; permission to use previously published materials included; and any advice given or actions advocated are solely the responsibility of the author, who assumes all liability for said work and indemnifies the publisher against any claims stemming from publication of the work.

RoseDog Books
585 Alpha Drive, Suite 103
Pittsburgh, PA 15238
Visit our website at www.rosedogbookstore.com

ISBN: 978-1-4809-8364-9
eISBN: 978-1-4809-8341-0

"Dr. Herron Gaston is an exemplary scholar, theologian, and social ethicist. His book focuses on the issues of mass incarceration and the daunting challenges formally incarcerated persons face when attempting to rebuild their lives. This book talks about the role of the church in addressing this tumultuous social conundrum and provides best practices for helping formally incarcerated individuals successfully transition back into their respective communities. The brilliance of this book should serve as a guide-post for those engaged in this transformational work of practically reversing the trends of mass incarceration."

Dr. Charlie Stallworth, Pastor, State Representative, Connecticut General Assembly

"Herron Gaston brings to this book an unusual combination of analytic insight into the dynamics of the criminal justice system with hands on experience in developing support for the formerly incarcerated as they re-enter their communities. Pastors, churches and community leaders will find here both the religious resources to mobilize in this effort and a fully practical tool to help them build realistic and effective ministries. A Call to Action shares wisdom from Gaston's leadership in his own congregation, whose activism in this area has been celebrated at both the city and state level. It also shares insights gleaned from other programs related to prevention and re-entry, inside and outside the churches."

S. Mark Heim
Samuel Abbot Professor of Christian Theology
Andover Newton Seminary at Yale
Visiting Professor of Theology at Yale Divinity School

ABSTRACT

The purpose of this project is to explore and establish a blueprint for United Methodist Churches based on the current Mission Plan for Restorative Justice Ministries (MPRJM). This Mission Plan could be used internally or externally within the United Methodist Church and beyond to begin to deal with the issues associated with the large numbers of persons leaving the prison system and reentering communities where the connectional system of the United Methodist Churches is established, and where other church denominations are in general, to assist retuning prisoners with reentry and restorative justice programs and ministries.

A call to action is for the United Methodist Church to use its historical work in this area along with its unique reformative connectional system. The United Methodist Church is poised to lead in this area because of its creed, structure, and connectional emphasis on mission work, outreach, and methodical steadfastness to deliver and foster justice and the restorative process among former prisoners. The Summerfield United Methodist Church Prison Reentry Model in Bridgeport, Connecticut was identified as one of the unique prison reentry and restorative justice type programs to further explore this initiative.

Using the Summerfield model as a starting point for this project, I invited parishioners to participate in focus group sessions in May 2017. A group of twenty-five parishioners of varying socioeconomic backgrounds volunteered to participate. The main discussion centered on our current prison fellowship ministry and whether members believed that we were making a difference in our own community. Following the focus groups, nine additional parishioners volunteered to further support this project with personal interviews, which took place between May and June 2017.

Results of the interviews were summarized and used to:

- Show support for the United Methodist Church's role in prison reentry and related ministries;

- Demonstrate consensus that more should be done, and what that "more" might look like; and
- Inform the contents of the Blueprint for Success, which could be used as a tool for initiating and/or enhancing programs for prison reentry ministry.

This project has implications for the ministerial practice for dealing with those who have transgressed — and how the United Methodist Church must use its spiritual and connectional resources to reform, redeem, and restore formerly incarcerated individuals back to God and to humanity.

TABLE OF CONTENTS

ACKNOWLEDGMENTS

I would like to take this moment to thank God for allowing me to engage in this academic endeavor. It has long been a goal of mine to complete my doctorate degree. Although my life has taken many twists and turns, I am deeply humbled that I have reached this very important milestone. I would like to thank everyone who has encouraged me along the way, who believed in me when I doubted myself. I owe my passion and character to my family, the most important people in my life. I especially thank my parents Moses and Mary Jasper-Gaston for being my number one cheerleaders. Without their words of affirmation and support I would not be blessed with such wonderful opportunities.

I thank my best friend, my brother-from-another-mother, Rodrick Spence, for his words of encouragement and for pushing me to burn the midnight oil to finish this very important task. I also acknowledge my church family, Summerfield United Methodist Church, for their steadfast commitment to my success and unequivocal support of me pursuing this degree and loving me unconditionally as their pastor. Additionally, I thank my many friends, fraternity brothers, and colleagues at Yale University, who offered me words of inspiration and hope in times when things seemed moot.

Moreover, a special thanks to my mentor and fraternity brother, Dr. Gregory J.

Harris, for reading my thesis, providing crucial feedback, helping with formatting, and for listening to me talk unceasingly about this topic every morning on my commute to work. Further, I would like to thank Dr. Sarah Drummond for affording me this incredible opportunity to apply and be accepted to this rigorous academic program. Sarah, believe it or not, you have been like an academic mother to me as I have engaged in critical reflection around this topic. A special thanks to Dr. Jenny Peace for her willingness to serve as my second reader for this project. I have enjoyed working with you and have greatly appreciated your benevolent and constructive feedback on ways to make my project as inclusive as possible. I am deeply grateful for your compassionate witness to radical inclusivity, love, and justice.

I appreciate each person in my life both past and present who has encouraged me in even the smallest way. I appreciate all my professors and teachers from grade school to college who have contributed to my scholarly pursuits and academic excellence.

A special thanks to Dr. Clifton Granby, Professor of Ethics at Yale University Divinity School, for his strong support and mentorship throughout this process. To my dear friend and clergy colleague, Rev. James Venable, for his words of wisdom and friendship down through the years. To my advisor, Dr. S. Mark Heim, for his fervent leadership and superb guidance in helping this to come to fruition, I am deeply grateful. Without your support, patience, and generosity this would not be made possible. Next, I would like to honor my dear fraternity brother, my fellow Christian, my fellow freedom fighter, and my fellow brother in the struggle for justice, Dr. Cornel West for his wisdom, guidance, and prophetic witness in demonstrating what it means to be a force for good and to stand in solidarity with those whose backs are against the wall. To Pastor

Donnie McClurkin, my spiritual father in the ministry, you have been such an incredible force of light and inspiration to me over this past year. I appreciate your words of encouragement, and thank God for our friendship.

Lastly, I would like to acknowledge and pay homage to my beloved grandmother, Lillia Mae Jasper-Booth, who told me as a child that I would pursue theological education and engage in the work of public religious life. Truly you were a prophet and the greatest earthly hero I have ever known, and I regret that you are not here in the flesh to see me walk across the stage to receive my diploma. But I shall never forget you, and you will live forever in my heart. This degree is for you as much as it is for me.

Introduction

Historically, religion has played an active role in almost every aspect of daily life in most societies since antiquity. As such, religion has been a dynamic force in transforming and restoring the lives of people throughout the world regardless of their transgressions. Likewise, religion has played an instrumental role in reconciling and healing the sinner, the sick, the destitute and those who have generally transgressed and moved away from God (Larson-Miller, 2015). Such practices of reconciliation, forgiveness, healing, and divine intervention are hallmarks of the Church's power and connection to God and faith. Further, the role of prayer and the power of the church to integrate these elements for citizens to live a full and complete life could possibly deliver a sinner to sainthood. While this power to heal, forgive, and reconcile is within the purview of the Church, many churches have not always reached out to the sinner or accepted the sinner with open arms, especially those who have been in the prison system and are released back to the community in an attempt to return to or begin a new life in God via the church.

Over the last decade, the challenges of reentry and other restorative justice measures and initiatives remain as dilemmas for many church denominations, individual church leaders and parishioners (Mears, Roman, Wolff & Buck, 2006). According to Durose, Cooper, and Snyder (2014), incarceration rates increased fourfold during the period from 1980-2006. It is estimated that 641,000 people leave prisons annually to return back to their respective communities (Wagner & Rabuy, 2017). In a recent report of mass incarceration, the Prison Policy Initiative (PPI) reported that the United States locks up more people per capita than any other nation in the world and it is estimated that the U.S. prisons hold approximately 2.3 million people for a variety of offences committed by youth, adults, men, and women in a variety of settings all over the country (Wagner & Rabuy, 2017).

This situation poses many challenges to the traditional church and denominational systems in America. Prisoners returning to society rarely find church programs or faith missions to restore and help individuals become productive citizens in society without ongoing persecution, shame, labeling, and castigation (Koschmann & Peterson, 2013). With such a large incarcerated population across America's prison system, it is estimated that 650,000 persons will be released annually and about twenty percent of them will return to urban areas; and most will be African American (Bureau of Justice Assistance, 2012).

The question is who will be there to receive them in a restorative fashion? The length of their imprisonment and the reason they entered the prison system may impact how families, friends, and communities receive them upon their exit from prisons back into the community. Many families may have abandoned them and friends may or may not be the best route, as relapses often occur which can land them back in the prison system. Recidivism rates are also at stake when prisoners try to reorganize their lives but have no alternatives or support to restore their lives and receive community and family support for change. Society in general may have already forsaken them. Theoretically, the Church is supposed to be the institution that should receive them, forgive them and move into the process of full restoration as God has restored us.

Statement of the Problem

People who commit crimes or sins according to human laws and laws of the Church are often condemned, alienated, or treated negatively. In essence, churches should do just the opposite. They should be engaged in the process of social justice, healing, forgiving, and eventual full restoration as Christ has mandated. More often than not, the negative labeling of the sinner by society and by the Church cripples and impedes the possibility for forgiveness, justice, and restoration within the Church or society. The double label of "sinner" and "felon" given by Church and society has often made it impossible for the sinner of any transgression to reconnect with God or the Church in order to be redeemed or liberated by the power and authority of the church. This issue becomes even more problematic when the person has committed some transgression against another person that falls within the framework of the Ten Commandments. Fundamentally, the lack of focus by many churches on social justice and restoration has added to the growing rates of recidivism once prisoners reenter the community, as there is little to no support for their true and positive reintegration back into society.

More serious crimes such as murder, theft, and other crimes against humanity are harder for the Church to accept and reconcile. It must be understood that churches have a fundamental theological responsibility not only to forgive and reconcile with the person but they must also restore him or her in a righteous and loving manner. This task becomes more complex as churches are being tasked with forgiving and reconciling sin among those who have been imprisoned and labeled in a negative fashion; and thus seen as a blight on society and marginalized. Not all church denominations are readily positioned or interested from a church polity standpoint to engage in this type of mission work and therefore many church communities and their members are not able to count on the Church to forgive, restore, or renew a person back to the Church, or in society or the community.

Purpose of the Project

The purpose of this project is to explore and establish a blueprint for United Methodist Churches based on the current Mission Plan for Restorative Justice Ministries (MPRJM) that can be used within the United Methodist Church and beyond to begin to deal with the issues associated with prison reentry and restorative justice. This urgent social justice problem of the faith community must be dealt with, given the growing number of persons incarcerated and those expected to return to communities where faith systems are located. The United Methodist Church, in particular, is poised to lead in this area because of its creed, structure, and connectional emphasis on mission work and, outreach to deliver and foster justice and the restorative process among former prisoners.

On this basis, its members can be trained and prepared from practical and theological standpoints to integrate prisoners back into the community (Petersen, 2002). This call to action must be met with the proper faith ingredients: justice, Christian love, forgiveness, reconciliation, and effective use of the power of God and prayer to liberate and re-integrate those who once transgressed back into society and back into the grace of God.

Guiding Questions for Call to Action

1 How can the United Methodist Church play a greater role in assisting with prison reentry and restorative justice?

2 How can the leadership and connectional mission of the United Methodist Church be used to create a blueprint for restorative justice programs through its connectional system?

3 What is the role of the leaders of the United Methodist Church in training, preparing, and empowering its laity for restorative justice and reentry activities within its current structure?

4 What should churches be trained to do in order to deal with prison reentry and restorative justice programs?

Justification for the Project

Regardless of the fact that many churches are involved with some degree of prison reentry and restoration programing, the United Methodist Church is better poised to provide the type of support, training, and theological basis for such initiatives, based on its 2004 Mission Plan for Restorative Justice

Ministries (MPRJM), and printed in the Book of Resolutions of the United Methodist Church (Cropsey & Minus, 2012).

First, the United Methodist Church's doctrine and polity support the concepts of justice and restoration and extend to those who for whatever reasons have strayed from God. As stated in the Mission Plan for Restorative Justice Ministries, the UMC supports restorative justice ministries and the belief that "justice is the basic principle upon which God's creation has been established." (p.29). Thus, justice is an "integral and uncompromising part of God's redemptive process, which assumes wholeness"; further, "compassion is characterized by sensitivity to God's justice and therefore, sensitivity to God's people" (p.29).

Second, the United Methodist Church acknowledges the current criminal justice system is a retributive justice system focused primarily on punishment. In contrast, the United Methodist Church's concept of dealing with prison reentry and related ministries is based on restorative justice, which has a message to its members and leaders that focuses on healing, making peace, and reconciling, thus transforming lives and healing people.

Finally, the United Methodist Church's unique connectional system, and integrated role within the communities it serves, better positions the United Methodist Church to make systematic change at all levels of the church itself and the community, through its strong outreach initiatives, support throughout the connectional system at the general church level, specific general church agencies, at the jurisdictional/central conferences, annual conference levels, and at the local level.

Position Statement of Researcher

At the commencement of my collegial academic journey at Florida A&M University, I became incredibly passionate about criminal justice reform in the State of Florida. This led me to become a lobbyist through Public Affairs Consultants, Inc., one of the state's largest lobbying firms tackling issues around immigration, education, and criminal justice reform. Through my lobbying efforts, I crafted a bill to dismantle the school-to-prison pipeline, particularly in Florida's inner-cities. I defended the proposal successfully before the Florida Legislature, and changes were enacted at the state level.

As a part of this incredible victory, I was offered a position in the Governor's Office to work directly with the Florida Department of Corrections on reentry initiatives for the State of Florida. My role was to help develop a best practice model of reentry to be replicated in other states throughout the United States. That same year, I was appointed by then Governor Charlie Crist to serve as the Co-chair of the Florida Council on the Social Status of Black Men and Boys. It was at this critical juncture in my career that I began to ask tough theological and philosophical questions around issues of justice, and I desired to wrestle with those questions in a rigorous academic setting, which led me to Yale Divinity School.

The questions by which I am most guided in relation to this subject are:

- What would it look like if the Church and the criminal justice system were in the business of restoring the relationships between the community, the victim, and the offender and invested in repairing the harm caused by crime instead of locking people up, throwing away the key, and resigning them to a perpetual state of systemic poverty?
- What should the moral and compassionate response of the church be towards formerly incarcerated individuals[1] be who have been relegated to the margins?
- What does reconciliation and unadulterated forgiveness look like in the context of the Church for those who have broken the law (whether biblical or secular), and what role does the Church have in restoring one back to one's respective community?

These questions guided my research interest and sustained me as a public intellectual and budding criminal justice reformer, and as a working theologian. During my first semester at Yale I experienced a tumultuous and life

---

[1] Whenever possible, I have tried to use the identifier "formerly incarcerated" as opposed to "prisoner." The term prisoner carries a connotation that people are no more than their actions, and is often digested and perceived in a way that says a person cannot be redeemed. By referring to people who have been in prison as formerly incarcerated, we maintain the societal and theological posture of reclaiming the person's humanity, of honoring them with the dignity and respect of which all human beings are worthy.

Dr. Herron Keyon Gaston

altering event. Prior to starting Yale in the fall of 2010, I worked at a youth camp in Tampa, FL, as a residence assistant. I was falsely accused of a crime, for which I was later arrested on Yale's campus. I found myself on the other side of prison bars. This experience enlivened me with rage, anger, disappointment, and sadness. For the first time I was experiencing the criminal justice system from the inside out, up close and personal. Therefore, I can speak to the realities of the criminal justice system from both sides, having served in a managerial capacity within corrections, and having been serviced by the correctional system as an inmate.

As a black man in America, I have experienced all too often the ease with which young men who look like me fall under the crushing yoke of injustice from an inherently biased criminal justice system. In twenty-first century America, the stakes are high and we must work indefatigably to put an end to the prison industrial complex, which ensnares disproportionately vulnerable communities of color. If you would like a full detail of my own personal experience with law enforcement and the criminal justice system, please consider purchasing my personal incarceration memoir entitled *The Darkest Night: An Incarceration Memoir, from Jail to Yale.*

This work is critical to the work of the Church because it is at the heart of the Gospel. Many biblical characters about whom we teach (e.g. Jesus, Paul, John, Peter,) in our modern context would be labeled "felons" and would be considered unredeemable for the infractions they committed against their respective societies. Yet these are exemplars we are taught to emulate. Therefore, as a church community, we must practice what we preach.

Behind the cell walls are fathers and mothers, sons and daughters, husbands and wives, friends and neighbors, sisters and brothers, rich and poor, black and white, and everyone in between. All of these persons are made in the perfect image of God and deserve a second chance.

Thus, I unequivocally believe that the United Methodist Church is uniquely equipped to lead the twenty-first century conversation across denominations and communities of faith around prison ministry. The ethos of prison ministry within the UMC tradition is to create a safer, more prosperous, spiritually renewed, fully reconciled community by providing spiritual and communal services for all parties (victim, offender, family), that leads to successful, long-term, and sustainable community reintegration and forgiveness.

Expectations from This Project

While the framework for this project is located within the tradition of the United Methodist Church, the work of ministering to formerly incarcerated persons crosses all lines of religious affiliation. The research, testimonials, call to action, blueprint, and even the specific program elements used in the Summerfield United Methodist Church program, are wholly transferrable to other traditions. The project has grown out of the UMC tradition, but is rooted in the Gospel values of serving those most in need – regardless of their social, economic, racial, education, or other status. As such, the ministry of Summerfield UMC, while certainly rooted in Christianity, is open to all persons who may need it. We do not require anyone to become Methodist, nor do we maintain any prescribed religious path for our program participants. Likewise, much of the work analyzed and presented in this project can be transferred easily to other Christian denominations, and may also be transferrable to Jewish, Muslim and other traditions, since the work builds on the interdependence of the human family – common to all religious paths, and even no religious path. One of the great impacts of this work would be for different faith traditions to unite in this work, creating faith-based community coalitions, and presenting a unified approach to prison reentry ministry that focuses on reclaiming the humanity and dignity of the formerly incarcerated.

Specific to the United Methodist Church, this project will help refine the current Mission Plan for Restoration Justice Ministries (MPRJM) and the UMC's connectional systems with a special emphasis on training and preparing the laity to integrate prisoners and others back into the church and to God. This project provides a strong and detailed blueprint for the United Methodist Church to expand its social justice and restorative principles throughout the nation and the world so that people of all walks of life will have the opportunity to experience God's social justice and redemptive grace

Dr. Herron Keyon Gaston

as they reintegrate back into the community. This project can serve as a model blueprint by operationalizing the Mission Plan for Restoration Justice Ministries (MPRJM) and can be used as a wake-up call for other faiths, denominations, and leaders to take up the mantle of forgiveness and re-establish God's plan for redemption, restoration, and healing back to the church and the faith community. This project helped me to reaffirm my own faith in God and my commitment to the United Methodist Church. It has helped me in my role as a practicing minister to accept, forgive, and restore community members who have been imprisoned and reenter the community as God would have me do.

CHAPTER ONE

Theological Framework for Prison Ministry and Reentry

Introduction

The purpose of this chapter is to provide a theoretical foundation for prison reentry and restoration by churches in general given the debate and issues associated with mass incarceration in the United States. This chapter will provide the theological and biblical basis for the role of the Church in moving toward ministries of prison reentry though the process of forgiveness, social justice, and the restoring of individuals back into the Church as well as their respective communities.

People may think Christian prison ministries serving those who have been otherwise marginalized in the larger society are relics of the past or are of no value or interest in the modern church of today. However, the Church has a long history of assisting and restoring people back to God and back to their respective families and communities through various strategies such as ministering to them, praying with and for them, and offering social service assistance. It is true that many churches, denominations, and their members have had different views about who should be restored, for what crimes or sins should they be restored, and even who should be responsible for restoring them. Nonetheless, the theological basis has always been part of the nexus of the Christian faith regardless of the interpreter or the interpretation, the punishment or the punisher.

Themes, and instances of justice, equality, and compassion are interwoven in the Bible and though God's encounter with humanity though Jesus Christ (Cleary, 2003).

These same themes and principles undergird the Mission Plan for the Restorative Justice

Ministries of the United Methodist Church (Cropsey & Minus, 2012). The Gospel of St.

Luke provides a framework for understanding social justice in Jesus's time and Luke's Gospel is often referred to as the social justice gospel due to its emphasis on Christian responsibility to the poor and disadvantaged (Carlson, 2016, p.16).

Therefore, it is vitally important to have a theological framework that embraces the characteristics and principles needed to assist those reentering the community from America's prisons who are plagued with complex needs for services and healing. This theological framework should also provide guidance for the application of these principles of justice and restoration within the halls of faith, principles that are sorely needed to bring healing and a seamless transition of integration back into the community.

This chapter will concentrate on the historical and biblical context of imprisonment and prisoners around a system of retribution. Additionally, I will consider how society and the church moved from more punitive orientations to that of social justice and restoration as preached and advocated by Jesus and his followers. This will be undergirded by the concepts and characteristics associated with prison theology (Pounder, 2008).

The Biblical Prison and Prisoners

There are many examples and references to prisons, prisoner confinement, and those expelled to live their final days in exile during biblical times, from the Book of Genesis in the Old Testament to Revelation in the New Testament. Many prominent and not so prominent people were imprisoned for a variety of crimes, sins, political and miscellaneous departures from the written and moral laws of the time, or perceptions of threats to the establishment. Marshall (2002) outlines that among prisoners of Biblical time, both of the

Old Testament and the New Testament, the Apostle Paul was probably the most noted and quoted prisoner. One must understand that the prison system of today is quite different than that of Biblical times. The prisons of Biblical times served primarily as holding tanks prior to an impending trial, which could lead to execution, exile, or even enslavement (Leviticus 24:12; Marshall, 2002; Numbers 15:34). Further, prisoners of Biblical times could also be detained or punished for unpaid debts, fines, or other economic factors. Griffith (1993) noted that prisons or cages have been used historically as sources of power and control, and as forms of governance.

Old Testament Themes of Prisons and Prisoners

The Old Testament of the Bible is replete with instances of imprisoned people who faced harsh penalties for any wrong-doing, or crimes against humanity or the Church. The strong notion of repentance and paying for your behavior and actions while in pursuit of peace and in carrying out the instructions of God are imbedded in the concept of Shalom. According to Strong's Concordance, Shalom is the Hebrew word which means peace, harmony, wholeness, completeness, prosperity, welfare, and tranquility. It is often translated as peace. The word is also used to greet people and bid them farewell as one departs.

Among the imprisoned, enslaved, or exiled people of the Old Testament were: Joseph who was refined by prison; Samson, who was chastened in prison; and Zedekiah, who was confined to prison until his death (Marshall, 2002). Additionally, the Bible gives several accounts in passages related to prisons in the Old Testament. Among them are:

And they put him in ward, that the mind of the LORD might be shewed them. (Lev 24:1)

And whosoever will not do the law of thy God, and the law of the king, let judgment be executed speedily upon him, whether [it be] unto death, or to banishment, or to confiscation of goods, or to imprisonment. (Ezra 7:26)

For the LORD heareth the poor, and despiseth not his prisoners. (Ps 69:33)

The Spirit of the Lord GOD [is] upon me; because the LORD hath anointed me to preach good tidings unto the meek; he hath sent me to bind up the brokenhearted, to proclaim liberty to the captives, and the opening of the prison to [them that are] bound. (Isa 61:1)

New Testament Themes of Prisons and Prisoners

The New Testament shares a unique attention to prisoners, prisons, and those persecuted for their faith or for challenging the government and laws. One could experience imprisonment and exile for various crimes, political unrest or insurrection, as well as the non-payment of taxes or debts, or openly criticizing the kings and leaders of the time. Several people in the New Testament were imprisoned, including: John the Baptist, Peter, James, John, Paul, Silas, Junia, Epaphras, Aristarchus, and certainly Jesus himself (Marshall, 2002). The Bible gives several accounts of such acts of imprisonment and the views of imprisonment during the New Testament era. Among them are:

- Naked, and ye clothed me: I was sick, and ye visited me: I was in prison, and ye came unto me. (Matt 25:36)
- Peter therefore was kept in prison: but prayer was made without ceasing of the church unto God for him. (Acts 12:5)
- Who, having received such a charge, thrust them into the inner prison, and made their feet fast in the stocks. (Acts 16:24)
- Him that is weak in the faith receive ye, [but] not to doubtful disputations. (Rom 14:1-23)
- Only let your conversation be as it becometh the gospel of Christ: that whether I come and see you, or else be absent, I may hear of your affairs, that ye stand fast in one spirit, with one mind striving together for the faith of the gospel. (Phil 1:27)
- Wherein I suffer trouble, as an evil doer, [even] unto bonds; but the word of God is not bound. (2 Tim 2:9)
- Remember them that are in bonds, as bound with them; [and] them which suffer adversity, as being yourselves also in the body. (Heb 13:3)

It is clear that Jesus wishes to reclaim those who had been imprisoned and to restore them back to a better state of being and humanity. Jesus seeks not only forgiveness but also restoration. The Apostle Paul is a prime example of the power of restoration. After his conversion he was not only forgiven by God for his many transgressions, including imprisoning and ordering executions of Christians, but he became a staunch supporter, minister, and writer about the Christian faith. He was imprisoned many times in different places and persecuted as he once persecuted other Christians (Marshall, 2002).

> After his conversion however, the imprisoner became the imprisoned, an experience which so stamped Paul's identity that he could refer to himself as a "prisoner of Jesus Christ" (Ephesians 3:1; Phlm 1:9). In 2 Corinthians, Paul speaks of enduring numerous "afflictions, hardships, calamities beatings, imprisonments, riots, labours, sleepless nights, hunger" (2 Corinthians 6:5; 11:2328). The book of Acts records Paul being locked up on three occasions – at Philippi, Caesarea, and Rome (Acts 16:19-40; 23:10; 24:27-28; 28:16.20.30). Paul was not alone in this experience. Peter and John were also repeatedly thrown in jail, and, like Paul, they too were sometimes busted out of jail by divine intervention (Acts 5:19, 22-23; 12:6-11; 16:25-26). The early church was actually led by a bunch of jail birds, and God was primary accomplice in their escape (Marshall, 2002, p.5).

Biblical Evidence of Prisons and the Christian Perspective

Marshall (2002) in his paper "Prison, Prisoners and the Bible," noted that the historical contexts of prisons and prison systems in Biblical times have great relevance for our modern criminal justice system. We must remember that prisons served different functions in Biblical times than they do today. We know today our prison and criminal justice system is ever changing, based on the political rule and emphasis of the day. It is also being driven largely by privatization and the prison industrial complex. It has already been noted by Marshall (2002) that crime is down, however the rise in incarcerations and building of prisons are up.

But, contrary to what most people think, our exploding prison population is not a symptom of increasing crime rates. There is not a one-to-one relationship between general crime rates and rates of imprisonment (although there is a closer relationship between rates of violent crime and rates of imprisonment). It is not crime rates so much as the community's general perception about crime, as reflected in social and political policy that accounts for the prison boom (Marshall, 2002, p.2).

Thus, Marshall (2002) observed four biblical accounts which held the differentiation between the prisons of Biblical times and those of today, and he explored how these can be applied today from a Christian perspective:

1 Imprisonment was a source of great suffering.
2 Imprisonment in biblical times was an instrument of oppression more than an instrument of justice.
3 Imprisonment is identified in scripture with the spirit and power of death.
4 God wants to set prisoners free.

Marshall (2002) further asserted that those who are engaged in working and dealing with the modern prison system should be sure to keep at the forefront three elements that are central to the Christian response:

1 *Care*: a focus on the New Testament teachings requires Christian believers to show care and concern for those in prisons. Remember those who are in prison, as though you were in prison with them; those who are being tortured, as though you yourselves were being tortured (Hebrews 13:3; Marshall, 2002, p.13).
2 *Critique*: we are called to evaluate prisons and the justice system critically, and equally to voice concerns about those

in jail, and decrease the increasing reliance in our society on prisons as a strategy for social control. "With the resurgence of retributivism in penal philosophy, the advent of the "prisonindustrial complex" in the commercial arena, and the ideological use of prisons to symbolize the authority of the state in the political sphere, prisons have become a self-sustaining growth industry (Cayley, 1998; Marshall, 2002, p.14).

3 *Community*: we are called to commit to the reintegration of released prisoners into "communities of care" (Marshall, 2002, p.15). People often defend prisons as a means by which offenders can "pay their debt to society". But the metaphor fails. Not only does society foot the bill for imprisonment but exprisoners are never really discharged of their debt. They bear a seemingly ineradicable stigma of having been inside (Marshall, 2002, p.15).

Consistent with the ideas of Marshall (2002), Garlitz (1993) recognized that the current system is broken and antiquated and must be replaced, and a paradigm change must replace the current retaliatory and punitive punishment system with one that is more restorative and imbedded in social justice.

Theological and Biblical Foundations of Restorative Justice

Restorative Justice entails a system of Shalom which includes principles of wholeness for individuals, relationships, and the community. Restorative Justice requires a complete understanding of the relationships that are affected by crime or other transgressions against persons, their families or society at large (Garlitz, 1993). In essence, restorative justice focuses on three basic tenets that are focused on authentically restoring the person within a Biblical context of care, since "God is a god of justice" (Garlitz, 1998, p.27) and those who subscribe to Christianity should also commit to adhering to the tenets of restorative justice principles (Garlitz, 1998). Following are the three core tenets of restorative justice, with accompanying Biblical accounts.

Crime results in injuries to victims, communities, and offenders. **The purpose of the criminal justice process should be to address and repair those injuries.** This tenet is based on Biblical principles of restitution, accountability, and forgiveness.

Restitution requires that offenders pay back or make whole the people who have been harmed by their actions. Specific biblical examples of the concept and use of restitution include the Mosaic Law, in Exodus 22, Leviticus, and Numbers 5; and the story of Zaccaeus in Luke 19. Restitution is a concrete reflection of the restoring of broken relationships (Garlitz, 1993), p.2).

Accountability is the expectation that a person must be ready to tell his/her story, to explain him/herself. There are many passages which reflect this principle by referring to a story as an account, either of a family (Genesis 10:1, Numbers 3:1) or of individuals (Genesis 6: 9). Psalm 10:13-15 refers to God holding a wicked person accountable. In Ezekiel 3:16- 1 9, God makes Ezekiel a watchman for the house of Israel and holds him accountable, not for Israel's response, but for his own actions. In Romans 3:9-20, Paul describes how the law makes us all conscious of sin and the whole world accountable to God. Accountability is a crucial element of recognizing and changing behavior which causes injuries (Garlitz, 1998, p.3).

Forgiveness is both a giving up of a claim to retribution and a ceasing to feel resentment about having been wronged. In Genesis 50:15-21 Joseph's brothers, who have sold him into slavery in Egypt, beg him to forgive them, and he reassures them of his forgiveness. In Matthew 18:21-35, Jesus teaches Peter that forgiving our brothers and sisters is central to restoring our relationship to our heavenly Father. Both of these passages describe relationships in which one party had been wronged, the offenders were held accountable and took steps to make things right, and the wronged party gave up their resentment and claims to retribution. Biblical forgiveness can be a very powerful tool in changing harmful behavior (Garlitz, 1993, p.3).

Essential to the Christian message are the concepts of forgiveness, mercy, and healing leading to reconciliation. This is what Jesus won for the human family on the Cross. These gifts form an essential part of what followers of Christ must practice in any age under all circumstances. The practice of forgiveness entails the conversion of peoples' hearts from anger, bitterness, hurt, and resentment to hearts of compassion, healing, and mercy. At the end of such a pathway lies true reconciliation. Within a retributive system of criminal justice there is little room for forgiveness or reconciliation. The victims of crime should not be excluded from the criminal justice processes. They need an opportunity to be heard and to access processes which would lead to reconciliation and healing. Too often offenders repeat their crimes, regardless of the social mayhem this causes. Victims often become embittered and harbor their anger, grief and pain for a lifetime. The community hardens its heart to offenders by demanding longer and harsher penalties (New Zealand Catholic Bishops Conference; Garlitz, 1993, p.3).

Not only government, but also **victims, offenders, and communities should be involved in the criminal justice process at the earliest point and to the maximum extent possible.** This tenet is based on several Biblical principles such as personal responsibility and worthiness/redemption.

Personal Responsibility allows people to answer for their actions, and lack of actions. In Genesis 16: 18-20, God commands that the Israelites appoint officials who are committed to justice, and warns how they will be held responsible for not following His commands. The prophet Isaiah warns of the many consequences of Israel's failure to meet its responsibilities to justice and righteousness. In Luke 11:46- 52, Jesus warns experts in the law that they are responsible for the actions of the generations who have gone before them, as well as their own. All those affected by crime are personally responsible to be actively involved in healing the injuries which result from crime (Garlitz, 1993, p.3). Cain tries to cover up his crime with a lie. This was and still is the case, when all kinds of ideologies try to justify and disguise the most atrocious crimes against human beings. "Am I my brother's keeper?" (Gen 3:9) Cain does not wish to think about his brother and refuses to accept the responsibility which every person has toward others (Garlitz, 1993, p.3).

Worthiness/Redemption is the promise that no one is beyond the reach of grace; no matter what we have done or failed to do, we are worthy to be an active participant in responding to crime. The Israelites who were redeemed from slavery in Egypt, even though continually failing to meet the responsibilities of their restored relationship to

God, were worthy to be active participants in establishing justice. The first chapter of Isaiah points out that God remains faithful and committed to restoring his broken relationship with people; God will restore judges and counselors (v.26), and Zion will be redeemed with justice (v.27). The epistle to the Galatians focuses on Christ's redemption of people into a restored relationship with God. All of those who are affected by crime are worth being redeemed, and have something to offer in healing the injuries which result from crime (Garlitz, 1993, p.4).

__In promoting justice, the government is responsible for preserving order, and the community is responsible for establishing peace.__ This tenet is based on Biblical principles of discipline, fairness, and reconciliation.

Discipline is training by instruction or exercise, most often to reinforce regularity, order, or rule. In Jeremiah 30:11, God declares that he disciplines, but only with justice. Hebrews 12: 5,6 states that the Lord disciplines those he loves, that God's discipline is an indication of our renewed relationship with him. The government has a responsibility to maintain order and work to prevent crime. Public authority must redress the violation of personal and social rights by imposing on the offender an adequate punishment for the crime, as a condition for the offender to regain the exercise of his or her freedom (Garlitz, 1993, p.4).

Fairness is a procedural aspect of justice which is often described as the quality of treating similar cases appropriately similarly and treating different cases appropriately differently. According to Psalm 9: 16, the Lord is known by his justice; Proverbs 1:3 and 29 describe the importance of fairness (Garlitz, 1993, p.5; Prison Fellowship, 2018). Traditionally in our society, the police are held responsible for maintaining law and order. This can only ever adequately be done when they have the respect of the community. That respect is in danger of being eroded if basic injustices are not tackled and if the police are called upon to maintain the law in situations of continued perceived injustice (New Zealand Catholic Bishops Conference; Garlitz, 1993, p.5).

Reconciliation is a restoration of right relationships, obtaining agreement and acceptance between parties, making paths congruous. In Isaiah 61, God anoints Isaiah to preach good news, to comfort all who mourn, to restore the places long devastated, to renew ruined cities, and to turn disgrace into rejoicing, because the Lord loves justice.

Second Corinthians 5:16-21 outlines the gospel of God's restoration of right relationships: God reconciled us to himself, and passed on to us this ministry of reconciliation. This reconciliation to God affects our relationships to our families and friends, and neighbors, and gives us a glimpse of the right relationships which still need restoration (Garlitz, 1993, p.5). An adversarial system by definition does not seek always to find the truth of a particular matter, but rather seeks a victory for one or other party. Such a system does not encourage offenders to take personal responsibility for their actions and can leave victims feeling that they are on trial, too. (Creating New Hearts – Journey From Retributive to Restorative Justice New Zealand Catholic Bishops Conference; Garlitz, 1993, p.5).

Prison Theology, Its Characteristics and Application

Pounder (2008) contends that prison theology is in essence a theology of liberation rooted in the Christian faith and functions and symbolizes the meaning of liberation for those people who have been oppressed in prison and by the criminal justice system. Pounder (2008) noted that it is important to understand the terminology associated with prison theology.

- *Prison* is defined as a "building or complex designated by law, for the confinement or detention of those persons who are judicially ordered into custody" (Pounder, 2008, p. 280).
- *Prisoner* is defined as "one who is confined in either a jail or prison or some other detention for some set amount of time" (Pounder, 2008, p.280).
- *Theology* is defined as that "ongoing activity of the whole church that aims at clarifying what "gospel" must mean here and now (Hall, 2003; Pounder, 2008, p.280).
- *Gospel* is defined two ways by Pounder (2008). The traditional way is the thought to reflect the "good news" of Jesus life, death, and resurrection, the empowerment of the Holy Spirit and the Trinity (Hall, 2003; Pounder, 2008, p.280).

Hall (2003) further asserts that the gospel betrays the true meaning of "evangellion," the Greek word translated as 'gospel' or 'good news.' Hall (2003) contends that "gospel is discovered, not possessed, and it is discovered in our struggle, as communities and persons of faith, to comprehend what is going on in our world (p.281).

Prison Theology as Contextual

According to Pounder (2008) prison theology is contextual because it seeks to determine the actual nature of the context and respond to that context from the Christian faith perspective. In other words, contextual theology seeks to find meaning in our Christian faith ethos and actions as they relate to the prison culture. It requires that Christians participate actively in the prison culture wherever people are involved in the criminal justice system (Pounder, 2008). This contextual concept takes on life when Christians go into the prisons to talk, counsel, minister, listen, share stories, and help to cultivate their own inner voices for change. Collectively, those imprisoned become connected to the outside world and particularly to those of the Christian faith. This contextual orientation also recognizes the strict boundaries that may contrain the prison guards and other officials as the Christian perspective is revealed and cultivated with the prisoner or inmate (Pounder, 2008). Pounder (2008) suggests that the prison theology has as its ultimate goal to:

> Immerse people into the reality of the oppression of prisoners and the system that enfolds them, and in that process, to motivate the church to recognize its liberation potential as both recipient and conveyer of concrete and specific gospel, good news, flowing from "the gospel" of the life, death, and resurrection of Jesus Christ, the empowerment of the Spirit and the work of our Triune God (Pounder, 2008, p.281).

Key Characteristics of Prison Theology

Pounder (2008) contends prison theology has three central characteristics, which are liberation, hope, and justice. There are five qualities of liberation as it relates to prison theology:

1. Liberation is characterized as the freedom from many things, but in the prison sense it refers to freedom from confinement or imprisonment.
2. Liberation means freedom from oppression and the oppressive systems of the criminal justice system.
3. Liberation means freedom from all the prison culture and physical and nonphysical elements that oppressed and caused emotional pain and suffering.
4. Liberation means freedom from the attitudes of the punisher and the system that created the oppressive bondage.
5. Liberation means to be free from rejection, marginalization, and being ostracized by family, friends, the system, and others.

Hope is the second component of prison theology and refers to the expectation that one can be liberated, able to express and experience freedom and hope in God and all things new as their lives are renewed (Pounder, 2008, p.283). In essence, hope symbolizes that Christ's cross and his suffering and eventual death and resurrection story can be our own story as we are liberated and have hope for a full and meaningful life. When a people or person has been freed from bondage, slavery, sickness, illness, or oppression they can regain hope though God's love and experience forgiveness (Pounder, 2008). This liberated freedom not only brings hope but it also allows us to abide in the presence of God and trust that God is always with you (Pounder, 2008, p.286).

Justice is the final aspect of the prison theology model which focuses on God's passion though Christians and others in society to use their influence, power, and resources to "affirm life" (Pounder, 2008, p.287). This aspect of prison theology requires that Christians discountenance evil, torture, isolation, deprivation, and other forms of severe and inhuman treatment of those imprisoned. Justice also requires that we indulge in a concerted effort to challenge laws, procedures, and policies that allow such torment or excessive punishment and treatment of prisoners (Pounder, 2008). Justice would also mean that the disparities and disproportionality around race and gender in the criminal justice system be reviewed constantly and energies devoted to uncovering and challenging the systematic persecution and disparate treatment of those traditionally marginalized groups in society (Pounder, 2008).

Theological Basis for Ministry

The challenge of some people being identified or labeled as worthy (the saved), and others as not worthy (the unsaved) continues to be a daunting hurdle for prison and reentry ministry. Theologians and those in ministry must be aware that "theological reflection must emerge out of ministry and for the sake of ministry if it is to be in accordance with the divine modality" (Anderson, 1979; Love, 2001, p.1). Thus, the work and mission of Christ and his life should be central to theology and an understanding of any ministry of humanity. Christ's life, ministry, death, and resurrection are imbedded in the struggle of humanity. His love and suffering are a theological testament to the prison ministry and therefore must be understood in that context. This is what Christians are called to do. They must aid and assist those who are poor, broken, destitute, and even imprisoned as Christ and so many others of Biblical times who believed in God and his Divinity. I posit that prison ministry and ministry geared at those on reentry into the community by the church is in essence Christian ministry. Watts (n.d.) asserted that any Christian ministry is the ministry of God in Christ and a mechanism of God's will, purpose, and faithfulness rather than of humans' needs, purpose, or technique. Watts noted that ministry is only ours because it is first God's and remains Christian as long as it remains God's.

All ministry done in the name and mission of God should be available to all peoples, regardless of their religious affiliation. Therefore, the church and its ministries must apply the theological foundations of ministry which are imbued and birthed from the Word of God and of his Holy power and Spirit to transfer this theology to the ministry or application of the church through its mission work and outreach. Prison ministry and reentry ministries within the church community must be understood from this fundamental position: that regardless of the transgression, crime, or sin committed, those who are of the Spirit of God must understand their mighty role as a human resource (Anderson, 1979). Byron Klaus (2011) produced several educational seminary lessons on the foundations of biblical theology and used the work of Anderson (1979) to create a series of lessons to demonstrate the vastness of biblical theology of ministry. The foregoing excerpts represent his outlook on theological ministry as informed by Anderson (1979). However, this might of human resources and human resoluteness is not a replacement or substitute for God's eternal resources, even though they are instruments to help alleviate pain and suffering in the present (Klaus, 2011).

The following passage from Matthew 7:21-23 explores this notion that our service to humanity as Christians must not be done for the sake of doing, but must be done with the full understanding and acceptance of the holy divinity and power of God's eternal purpose for humanity. "Not everyone who says to me, Lord, Lord, will enter the

Kingdom of heaven, but only he who does the will of the Father who is in heaven. Many will say to me on that day, Lord, Lord did we not prophesy in your name and in your name drive out demons and perform many miracles? Then I will tell them plainly, I never knew you. Away from me you evildoers!"

Klaus (2011), as cited in Anderson (1979), suggested several Biblical clues to remind us of God's power, authority, and mission work through humanity:

- "God is at work." (p.8). (John 5:17)
- "God continues to empower His redemptive spirit mission." (p.8). (Acts 1:68)
- "Pentecost is the guarantee that the Jesus of the Gospels is the Jesus who continues His ministry empowered by the Holy Spirit." (p.8). (Acts 2:22-24)
- "Our ministry is the continuing ministry of Christ working through us by the presence and power of the Spirit of Christ." (p.8). (2 Cor 5:20)

Klaus, informed by Anderson, further asserted that the gift of discernment allows us to have enough spiritual maturity to know the difference between works of human effort and the continuing ministry of Jesus empowered by the Spirit.

- "Discernment assumes the present tense of Jesus' redemptive ministry." (p.10)
- "Discernment assumes that Christ's Kingdom rule extends over all human structures and efforts." (p.10)
- "Discernment strives to "see" the presence of Jesus in all ministry actions and structures and not as an act of piety, but as a biblical necessity." (p.10).

Klaus also highlighted key factors regarding the relationship between discernment and "True Ministry."

- "A connectedness to the life of Jesus." (p.11). (John 15)
- "An affirmation that holiness and ethics are never mutually exclusive." (p.11). (2 Cor 5:20)
- "A willingness to exegete ministry contexts with the same rigor we exegete biblical texts." (p.12). (Matt 7:21-23)
- "A commitment to evaluating ministry methodology by whether or not it facilitates Jesus' continuing redemptive ministry." (p.12).

Anderson's (1979) theological contributions to our thought process and mission work, as elaborated on by Klaus (2011), are crucial to understanding "the task of working out a theology for ministry" (p.18). Accordingly, Klaus believed Klaus believed that this chore begins with the task of identifying the nature and place of ministry itself, prioritizing the Bible as the original authority of faith, yet balancing the biblical text with a deep understanding of context, both historical and contemporary (p.18). For Anderson, theology for ministry means that all ministry is first and foremost God's ministry, and that every act of revelation is a ministry of reconciliation that can be seen and understood within the context of prison reentry ministry (Klaus, 2011). Klaus (2011) reminds us that in essence, "ministry should precede and produce theology, not the reverse" (p.19).

The Theology of Sadie Pounder and Christopher Marshall

Sadie Pounder (1946-2014)

The late Sadie Pounder's (2008) work with prison ministries in the U.S. within the Lutheran tradition is buttressed by her background in counseling and her personal ministry and theology around the goals of God's promise of liberation, hope, and justice. She believed that the church is called and mandated to deliver those in prison and those who reenter their respective communities to be liberated and freed of oppression and oppressive manifestations (Pounder, 2008). These expectations are carried out by those inspired and influenced by the Word of God. This theological ministry of liberation for all people who have been oppressed include "feminist, Black, womanist and Latino/Hispanic movements" (p.278). She noted that prison ministry is not in and of itself, prison theology. However, "it is a dynamic way of life intended to free the oppressed from the dehumanizing mental, emotional, physical, and spiritual bondage that accompanies imprisonment and the entire criminal justice system" (Pounder, p.288). Pounder (2008) hoped that the church would recognize and be compelled "to build a bridge not for them but with them (p.289). Pounder (2008) felt that the time was now and we should all care, but especially those of the faith of God (Nolan, 2004). While Pounder (2008) focused mainly on those in prison and the accompanying issues around family dynamics, she was aware of the issues associated with reentry. However, most of her work and theological emphasis was on helping those who were oppressed by the bondage of prison and the prison culture. These ideas and theological foundations associated with God's Word and His call for humanity to respond are imbedded in the hope of justice, and compassion.

Christopher D. Marshall (1953-   )

The lifelong work of Christopher Marshall (2002) has emphasized Christian studies in New Zealand at all levels. Marshall has worked nationally and internationally to help translate theory into personal practice in the areas of restorative and social justice by focusing on six principles that combine spirituality, theology, and action: presence, conviction, content, respect for students, preparation, and delivery. He has written extensively about how the Kingdom of God imbedded in society must move beyond systems of retribution and move closer to a new vision for justice through restoration. Marshall's work and writings in the area of human rights are a testament to his interest in the need for a paradigm shift from retributive and punitive systems to systems that are more forgiving. Marshall (2002) also focused on the role of the church and Christians to take the lead in reducing suffering and working collectively as those of the faith to restore people who once transgressed or sinned back to their communities. Marshall (2002) explained that we often see prison as a way of people paying their debt to society through long-term imprisonment and suffering the many atrocities therein. But, in fact, he contends that society actually pays the debts after prisoners are freed and attempt to reenter the community, because they are often so stigmatized that they are not able to get jobs or cannot seem to get beyond their label as a criminal (p.15).

Marshall's (2002) theological orientation is rooted in the fact that Christians must direct their attention and efforts into greater peacemaking and restoration of prisoners and those entering back into their communities, rather than on further negative labeling, marginalization, and retribution (p.15). This reintegration movement and a focus on after care would require a commitment to the fostering of "communities of care" (p.15). Thus, Marshall (2002) recognized the following mandate of Christians:

> What former prisoners need most is a community of people who truly understand both the grace and the discipline of forgiveness, a community that loves its "enemies" and welcomes strangers, a community that breaks down the dividing walls of hostility and preaches "peace to those who

were far off" (p.15). Accordingly, "this what Christ did, and this is what those who bear his name should also do" (p.15; Eph 2:14-17).

Differences and Similarities of Pounder and Marshall

While there are many similarities between Pounder's (2008) and Marshall's (2002) theology of prisoners and the role of Christians, they have some basic theological differences. They are similar in defining the role of Christians and the church as taking charge of the monumental task of loving, forgiving, and reintegrating; where they differ somewhat is in their approaches. Pounder (2008) clearly explored the roles of the church and Christians to liberate and free the oppressed from a culture of poverty, prison, and bondage of any kind. She recognizes that oppression can impact many types of people, but there are some groups in society that are more likely to be subject to this evil. She proposed a ministry and a theology around liberation, hope, and justice which can be compared loosely to Marshall's (2002) theology of expressions of generosity and hospitality to those who are behind bars, requiring that we must understand that grace and forgiveness are necessary ingredients to express love to your enemies and welcomes strangers back upon reentry into the community (p.15).

Narrow Divergence of Justice and Its Implication

Though the differences are few between Pounder and Marshall, the real significant differences are in Marshall's (2002) emphasis and extension of the "justice" component of prison theology. As mentioned earlier, both Pounder (2008) and Marshall (2002) support the basic elements of prison theology as a form of justice and social reformation where the prisoner is reintegrated back into the society of God, in contrast with human society which may continue to punish, limit, and control even after prisoners have paid their confinement and monetary debt to society. Rather, Pounder (2008) and Marshall (2002) suggest those who are of the Christian faith be prepared to forgive, restore, and reintegrate the prisoner back into society for multiple Biblical and Christian principles around God's love, forgiveness, and hope for humanity in His likeness.

The divergence between the two lies in Marshall's reliance on a more "social justice" model or paradigm. This model applies not only to the role of the church. The entire criminal justice system can see greater gains and even reductions in crime and recidivism if this model can be adopted throughout the criminal justice system. It is clear that both of these scholars believed that though Christ suffered for our sins, it was not his goal for this type of great suffering caused by human hands to be continued in the criminal justice system. Marshall (2002) is clear in that "prisons hurt and contradicts humanity" (p.6). This idea of Christ who was set-free from the dead by God's Divine power gave humanity the roadmap for the humanitarian treatment of all people who are made in the likeness of God, resonates in this ideology. Marshall (2002) details what this social justice paradigm entails more than Pounder does. Pounder (2008) has a more global all-inclusive view of justice as not only correcting a wrong in society. She also integrates concepts of liberation (freedom), and an eschatological state of hope. This hope according to Pounder (2008) is embedded in God's highest form of love and charity bestowed upon humanity. This hope of the cross is a symbolic representation of a defiance against death in the literal and figurative sense. All of which Christ endured for our ultimate freedom from sin and death, regardless of the circumstances in which we find ourselves.

Marshall (2002) more clearly commits his dialogue and theology to the community's role in the work of prison reentry through reintegration into communities of caring contexts. He notes that the community must embrace God's forgiveness in a way that enables them to truly love its enemies and even those who may have committed heinous crimes against society and humanity, but who must be forgiven, because this is what Christ did and therefore expects of each of us.

The implications of Marshall's (2002) deeper expectation and commitment to the whole community changing its negative perspectives and prejudices against prisoners would require a complete overhaul of the criminal justice system at every level. That overhaul would oblige the system to retrain and recommit its workforce to engage in more rehabilitation, reform, and peacemaking techniques in which those in the criminal justice system, the offender, the victim, and the community, enter into a formal committed relationship with rights and responsibilities (Chong, 2006). Other implications associated with Marshall's (2002) position include the connection to God's laws and legislation inherent in the Torah and his love and compassion for the poor, sick, and down-trodden. Jesus Christ's life, death, and resurrection is a symbol of our duty to engage in social justice strategies that are reformative, restorative, and redemptive.

Primacy of Prison Theology of Pounder
with the Restorative Justice Principles of Marshall

I propose the integration of Pounder's (2008) prison theology as liberation theology (and its components of hope and justice) with the restorative justice principles of Marshall (2002) and his notions of freedom as expressed biblically internally and externally through God's commitment to set prisoners free (p.12). Marshall (2002), like Pounder (2008), recognized the power of God's Word and the role of Christian mission to help usher in moral and spiritual liberation even when people are physically detained and internally troubled. This idea is germane to prison ministry which Marshall (2002) and Pounder (2008) both support and recognize as meaningful sources of support and Christian love. They also believe that believers must work hard to help prisoners in their efforts to be released and "support them through post-release adjustment as the consummation of the freedom Christ brings" (p.12). Furthermore, both Pounder (2008) and Marshall (2002) affirm that mercy, repentance, and restoration are key elements to a successful transformation. Therefore, I contend that the integration of these ideas best support the foundation of the blueprint, as it must have these elements and be guided by the Word of God and the Holy Spirit.

Summary

This chapter sought to provide a theological and biblical overview for prison reentry and restoration by churches in general given the debate and issues associated with mass incarnation in the past and in the modern era. A special focus was placed on the fundamental tenets of restorative justice and the use of prison theology as a foundation for changing the lives of those imprisoned and empowering the faith community to make every effort to free those in bondage internally and externally.

CHAPTER TWO

The Complexities of Mass Incarceration, the Prison Industrial Complex, and Faith-Based Community Reentry

Introduction

The purpose of this chapter is to situate the project within current theological and academic research and practice around prison reentry, mass incarceration, the prison industrial complex, and the role of the Church in general and the United Methodist Church in specific. The first goal of this chapter is to define and understand the current debate regarding mass incarceration and prison reentry in the context of the prison industrial complex structure within the United States and the scholarship in that area. The second goal is to shed light on the problem associated with recidivism rates in the U.S. and how this breeds a revolving door effect in society, using this information as a platform for the Church to intervene and support prison ministries in general, and reentry and restorative justice programs in specific. The third goal is to focus on the Church as a social justice agent and as a forgiving and reconciling body for those who have been imprisoned and are returning to the community. The fourth goal is to explore the role of the United Methodist Church in preparing its membership to play an active and leading role in prison reentry and to claim its mission as a reforming, redeeming, and restoring institution to assist in making an impact on prisoners' transition to restoration.

Mass Incarceration Defined

Garland (2001b) originally coined the term mass incarceration to describe a clear expansion of imprisonment within the United Sates between 1975 and the 1990s. This new prison management phenomena consisted of polices and politics favoring imprisonment to create safety, security, and control. Additionally, the new focus on imprisonment favored raising the cost of crime, both monetarily in terms of bail as well as in terms of the overall effect on one's life through higher punishments. These costs disproportionately affect the criminally predisposed, those already a part of the criminal justice system; and the more historical criminal populations, those who because of their race or income have been identified as having a greater inclination toward criminal activity and are therefore targeted by the criminal justice system. While some argue that this system of massively incarcerating groups of people is mostly political, few would agree on its scientific basis (Garland, 2001b; Wacquant, 2009; Western, 2006).

Nonetheless, this topic has marshaled much debate about mass incarnation and what seems to be the labeling, targeting, and controlling of certain subpopulations within the United States. African Americans have been largely associated with being the targets for imprisonment in this country on a massive scale even as we have witnessed decreases in overall crime. Based on data from the U.S. Department of Justice (USDOJ), the Pew Trust (2016) reported that over the period from 2010 to 2015 the imprisonment rates fell 8.4 percent while the combined violent and property crime rate fell by 14.6 percent. Additionally, the report noted that rates of violent and property crimes reported to law enforcement both have declined by half since their 1991 peak.

Yet, there is still debate about why African Americans in general, and African Americans males specifically, seem to be more disproportionately represented in the criminal justice system at all levels, thus contributing to the phenomena of massive incarceration and fueling the prison-industrial complex. Disproportionate minority contact (DMC) refers to the disproportionate number of minority youth who come into contact with the criminal justice system compared with their percent of the overall population (Office of Juvenile Justice and Delinquency Prevention, 2012). Alexander (2010) and Forman (2012) represent two different positions on this phenomenon of declining crime rates coupled with the seeming increase in African American imprisonment via the mass incarceration narrative.

The Alexander and Forman Debate

Michelle Alexander (2010) contends that the problem of mass incarceration is imbedded in our racial-caste past driven by the power of politics, social control, and the vestiges and hostility of slavery. She contends that many would prefer not to engage in a discussion about race as some would like to believe we have moved past race as a problem in our modern era to a new phase of "colorblind justice." According to Alexander (2010) this notion of post-racialism in the U.S. and even around the globe is essentially fiction. She asserts that we still live in a racial caste social structure and this is apparent throughout our criminal justice system through the mass incarceration of the subpopulation of poor people of color. Accordingly, Alexander (2010) posits that mass incarceration is the equivalent of a new caste system fueled by socio-political and economic factors in our modern era. She contends that mass incarceration as a system is the "New Jim Crow," as was the so-called "War on Drugs" (p.7). Like the "Jim Crow" system post-slavery in the U.S., Alexander (2010) discovered that this was a system like no other where there was a systematic clear goal to detain, control, and interfere with the normal rights and movements of an entire group of people.

Jim Crow was based largely on race and fear, and constituted through the laws of local and state governments in the South between 1877 and the beginning of the civil rights movements in the 1950s to continue the segregation and disenfranchisement of African Americans. Alexander contends that the old Jim Crow was fueled by race and supported by laws as a form of control to separate blacks from whites while reminding blacks of their inferior status. This new system of mass incarceration is the modern era's post racially disguised effort to do the same thing. This system of mass incarceration is therefore the New Jim Crow. The criminal justice system is the comprehensive system that carries out the same types of atrocities as the old Jim Crow's system did in America's dark racially charged past. The criminal justice system is the new agent that labels people of color as bad, criminal, and not worthy of the freedoms naturally granted others.

Overall, Alexander (2010) asserts that we have not ended the old Jim Crow post slavery but reinvented it through the criminal justice system. Its detrimental effects can be seen through the incomprehensible system of mass incarceration within the criminal justice system. Alexander (2010) used a variety of comparative data points to analyze the disparate and differential treatment of people of color, specifically African American males, throughout the criminal justice system, supporting her assertion of a camouflaged system.

On the other hand, James Forman (2012) argues that Alexander's (2010) thesis of the New Jim Crow is inherently flawed. He maintains that the New Jim Crow framing or analogy gives an incomplete picture of mass incarceration (Forman, 2012; Stephens, 2015). Forman (2012) therefore asserts that one must understand mass incarceration's historical origins, black attitudes toward crime and punishment, the ignoring of violent crimes and the focusing primarily on drug crimes, differences in class distinctions, and the impact of mass incarceration on other racial groups.

While Forman generally accepts many of the factors associated with a historical and traditionally racially-based society, and understands disparities and differential treatment of different groups of people in the criminal justice system on a variety of measures, he feels that the New Jim Crow analogy may somehow incompletely tell the real story of why and how mass incarceration came into existence and why it persists. Forman (2012) who has written extensively about the punitive and extensive nature of the criminal justice policies and mass incarceration is also morally and professionally opposed to the nation's criminal justice issues that seem to disproportionality impact people of color. Forman (2012) credits Alexander (2010) for detailing and illuminating comprehensively the New Jim Crow thesis in the literature but critiques it at the same time because it over-emphasizes the War on Drugs. Forman (2012) notes that this would not be an accurate claim since drug offenders make up a quarter of the nation's prisoners and violent offenders make up a much larger portion. By not looking closer at the role of violent crimes, as seemed to be ignored by Alexander (2010) in her thesis of the New Jim Crow, we miss a major piece of the explanatory puzzle of the response to mass incarceration. Additionally, the punitive approach to violent crimes and even some drug offenses need to be countered with a less punitive approach than currently used in our country.

Forman (2012) notes that in order to understand mass incarceration and all its dimensions, one must take into account drug and violent offenders, and white prisoners, who are largely invisible and are somewhat omitted in the discourse by Alexander (2010). Forman (2012) feels that in much of the racial connection with mass incarceration, the New Jim Crow authors overlooked two critical factors: crime had already increased before the beginning of the prison boom (Garland, 2001), and street crimes had quadrupled between 1959 and 1971 (Forman, 2012; LaFree, 1998). He suggests given these two critical points, the New Jim Crow writers chose to ignore those facts, rather they based their claims on a controversial Federal Bureau of Investigations report (Alexander, 2010; Forman, 2012).

Moreover, Forman (2012) noted additional flaws with the New Jim Crow argument. He argues that many black activists, the NAACP leaders, and many residents of large metropolitan areas are encouraging police to get tougher on crime and in some cases called for tougher sentences and more police presence. These accounts according to Forman (2012) are largely ignored, absent, and not introduced to the discourse. In essence, Forman (2012) contends that not only have whites supported or added to the problem of mass incarceration, but blacks have also contributed to this system as active citizens in many communities who vote and exercise authority over the types of neighborhoods, and the level of safety they wish to enjoy. Blacks enjoy majority voting areas and can determine who they wish to have represent them as well as protect them in terms of public safety. In essence, there are a number of blacks who support tough crime laws.

Further, Forman (2012) suggests that the New Jim Crow writers disregard the violent crimes committed by blacks and simply focus on the laws around the differential treatment of drug offenses by race and even geography associated with the War on Drugs which many believe to be a form of Jim Crow disguised as a way to eradicate drugs in the U.S. Forman (2012) considers this to be a major omission of key facts about violent crimes rates committed by blacks. He supported this characterization by noting that blacks are overrepresented in the category of violent crimes with arrest rates seven to eight times higher than the white arrest rate; "the black arrest rate for robbery is ten times higher than the white arrest rate" (Forman, 2012, p.42; Ruth & Reitz, 2006). While the data continues to support a disproportionate violent crime rate for blacks, Foreman (2012) notes the sensitivity of this issue as a human phenomenon is understood, but to omit it, as the New Jim Crow authors do, does not get to the root of mass incarceration.

The New Jim Crow authors have also obscured the role of class, especially when comparing middle and upper-class blacks to whites. The thesis that the New Jim Crow of mass incarceration only affects poor, uneducated, and marginalized blacks does not fit well with the fact that many black, well-educated, and middle and upper-class people also suffer disparate treatment; however, the more educated you are the greater your life chances and the less likely you are to get arrested. Forman (2012) suggests a clear omission by Alexander (2010) and others who support the New Jim Crow: welleducated, high income blacks also have privilege and not all blacks experience the same treatment as poor, less-educated blacks do and are less likely to add to the mass incarceration population.

Finally, Forman (2012) suggests that Alexander (2010) ignores race, to the extent that whites too contribute to the mass incarceration as targets. The notion that whites are not arrested and detained for a variety of crimes is not an accurate and full account and thus views mass incarceration as a "black thing." Forman (2012) points out that many poor, uneducated and disadvantaged whites are also behind bars and that at least one third of the national prisoners are white. According to Forman (2012) the plight of Latino prisoners is also ignored in the New Jim Crow position as many Latino citizens have been disenfranchised as many blacks have.

These and other omissions around race, class, and the role that blacks play in mass incarceration are largely missed in this New Jim Crow narrative of Alexander (2010) and other writers. Forman (2012) certainly believes that there does exist disproportionality and an over-representation of African Americans at all levels and that would include other people of color in our country. He contends that that is not the whole story, nor does the label of the New Jim Crow as coined by Alexander (2010) and other writers best capture the complexities of mass incarceration.

Integrating the Perspectives of Alexander and Forman

Both authors have great points and respond to the issue of mass incarceration in a comprehensive manner. The thesis by Alexander (2010) creates a very meaningful and compelling link to the vestiges of slavery, racism, and the War on Drugs with the new preoccupation with crime as a way of marginalizing, labeling, and subjecting people of color to a new form of Jim Crow called mass incarceration. While this is a strong argument, Forman suggests not using the term "New Jim Crow" because it omits other key factors that add to the problem of mass incarceration in our country. Therefore, I recommend an integrated approach to understanding mass incarceration as a function of many factors suggested by Alexander (2010) and Forman (2012) which has led to a complex economic system to sustain a capitalist society while missing opportunities to invest in the families, communities, and to begin to re-think our system of justice, punishment, and retribution to a more humane system of social justice as posited by Pounder (2008) and expanded upon by Marshall (2002).

After considering both Alexander's and Foreman's arguments regarding mass incarceration, I tend to be more persuaded by the case that Alexander makes in asserting that mass incarceration is the New Jim Crow. My agreement with her rests on the general understanding that the American experience for marginalized groups of people, who are often poor and black, have far-reaching implications and repercussions. As such, the entire American project serves to benefit and advance the dominant group in society, while bastardizing the marginalized, the disposed, and the poor. This class system has deep racial ramifications that impact every aspect of one's existence. The bastardization process of reducing one's humanity serves to dehumanize an entire group of people, and, therefore, the dominant group is given leverage to set rules and polices that work to their advantage. This means that the dominant group are bestowed certain entitlements that may or may not be afforded to other groups in the same way. For example, if one is financially secure and white, one can pay one's way through the judicial system rather effortlessly. Furthermore, this level of entitlement allows white individuals not to have to worry about walking down the street and looking suspicious, walking into a supermarket and being pursued by security, attending an elite institution and not having one's merits questioned, or committing a white-collar crime and being labeled a "super-predator."

I think regardless of how one chooses to examine the issue of mass incarceration, one cannot overlook the fact that racism and racist policies play a pivotal role in creating disparities. I argue that racism cannot be omitted when examining the issue of mass incarceration. In my opinion, Foreman attempts to placate and sanitize the issue that race plays in perpetuating mass incarceration. While he purports to understand Alexander's position, he accuses her of giving people an incomplete picture of what was taking place in American society in the 1960s and early 1970s. Foreman argues that at the beginning of the prison boom, violent crimes had already shot up drastically. During the period between 1965 and 1975 homicide rates and robbery rates skyrocketed. Foreman, therefore, concludes that there was a demand for more punitive policies. In other words, it almost seems as if Foreman is blaming the black community for its own issues around mass incarceration as if they helped to bring this upon themselves. While he may not be saying this directly, he seems to hint at this idea by pointing out Alexander's perceived blind spots.

When Foreman makes the case in his argument that Alexander does not pay close enough attention to the white prisoner population, he distracts from the heart of the issue that Alexander is making. I think that her project is intentional in not engaging the nuances of the white prison population – because she is demonstrating that there is a disproportionate number of people of color behind bars due to the undercurrents of unfair policies which ensnare and entrap poor communities of color. She asserts that this disproportion boils down to the way in which we police certain communities, and the general perceptions of who fits a criminal profile. Alexander has a specific project in mind, I would argue, and her research is squarely around incarceration issues affecting the black community. It is not my intention to argue for "oppression Olympics," that is, to argue that one person's suffering is gold medal suffering and others' suffering is less. However, I do recognize

Dr. Herron Keyon Gaston

the "oppressive minority" status experienced through our criminal justice system based on race, ethnicity, and socioeconomic factors. Yet, I worry about the danger of conflating related but distinct expressions of discrimination by drawing in a broader audience without the author's invitation.

I would like to stress the need for a truly intersectional approach to understanding mass incarceration and how it affects other groups outside of Black Americans, but I don't want the issue to become a sidebar conversation instead of the central focal point. So often the latter happens. What Forman's argument does when he draws in other groups, in my opinion, is pitting other minority groups (i.e. Hispanics) against each other (blacks), and there is a real danger there. I would like to raise awareness of how violent that can be in a community. But, certainly, I appreciate his position and voice on the matter.

The Core Problem of Mass Incarceration and the Prison Industrial Complex

The United States has the largest prison population in the world, housing approximately 1.8 million people in some form of custody with 100,000 in federal prisons, 1.1 million in state prisons and 600,000 in local jails. Marc Mauer in his book *The Race to Incarcerate* (2006) argues that America appears to have made a concerted effort to detain more people than any other nation in human history, which has resulted in a variety of challenges for all segments of life. Regardless of the gains made in America by African Americans in particular, the statistics seem alarming as to what can be expected to befall many African Americans and their families via the criminal justice system and an ethos and desire to incarcerate even when crime rates seem to be on the decline nationally (Mauer, 2011). Mauer noted a historical precedent for the increasing mass incarceration, and differential and unequal treatment in America particularly among African Americans within the criminal justice system:

> In 1954, the year of the historic Brown v. Board of Education decision, about 100,000 African Americans were incarcerated in America's prisons and jails. Following that

decision, there has been a half century of enhanced opportunity for many people for whom it had previously been denied, and significant numbers of people of color have gained leadership positions in society. Yet, despite this sustained progress, within the criminal justice system, the figure of 100,000 incarcerated African Americans has now escalated to nearly 900,000. The scale of these developments can be seen most vividly in research findings from the Department of Justice. If current trends continue, 1 of every 3 African American males born today can expect to go to prison in his lifetime, as can 1 of every 6 Latino males, compared to 1 in 17 White males. For women, the overall figures are considerably lower, but the racial/ethnic disparities are similar: 1 of every 18 African American females, 1 of every 45 Hispanic females, and 1 of every 111 White females can expect to spend time in prison). Available data, though, documents that Native Americans are incarcerated at more than twice the rate of Whites, while Asian Americans/Pacific Islanders have the lowest incarceration rate of any racial/ethnic group (Mauer, 2011, p.296).

Garland (2001b) first introduced the concept of mass incarceration to describe a distinctive pattern of expansion of imprisonment in the United States. He characterized mass incarceration in the following manner:

>...mass imprisonment constituted a new regime of penalty that differed along two dimensions from varying policies of imprisonment in use by modern societies since the end of the eighteenth century. First, U.S. imprisonment rates in the late 1990s marked a substantial departure from historic norms for the scale of imprisonment during the twentieth century by several magnitudes. Second, in contrast to a history of using imprisonment against individuals based on crime and criminal history, contemporary mass imprisonment reflected

Dr. Herron Keyon Gaston

a "systematic imprisonment of whole groups of the population" (Garland, 2001b, p.228).

Other terms such as "hyper incarceration" as coined by Wacquant (2009) have also been used to encapsulate the dramatic change in the scales of imprisonment, imprisonment that has not been equally distributed as would be implied using the term mass incarceration (Garland, 2001b; Wacquant, 2009). Wacquant (2009) contends that "hyper incarceration" may better capture the unequal distribution of certain groups in society most at risk of incarceration such as those with less than a high school education, African Americans and Hispanics. According to Garland (2001b) this public policy shift bred a social problem in the American society of paramount concern to all segments of society. Several broader causes cited by some for this rise in incarceration are high anxiety societies, racialized threat and animus, neoliberalism, and the politics associated with crime and control (Garland, 2001b).

Mass incarceration statistics reveal that persons of color, primarily African Americans, are experiencing more racially disproportionate contact with the criminal justice system even in the wake of declining crime rates (Western & Wildeman, 2009). Garland (2001b) and Wacquant (2009) suggest the impact falls on some groups more than others in society. Most often these are groups that have traditionally been discriminated against and targeted for differential treatment in the United States. Western and Wildeman (2009) contend that the penal system in America inherently supports social and economic divisions, as men, women, blacks, and whites experience the impact of mass incarceration differently. These authors suggest a causal relationship by those who have power within political, governmental, and criminal justice structures to control, oppress, alter, and make decisions about the activities, behaviors, and daily lives of certain groups of people in our country. The differences and disparities appear to be well documented and authenticated as indicated by Western and Wildeman (2009). Western and Wildeman make reference here to the demographic situation of the penal system in American and suggest that men, especially white men of economic advantage, seem to move through the criminal justice system with more ease than other populations:

The broad significance of the penal system for American social inequality results from extreme social and economic disparities in incarceration. More than 90 percent of all prison
and jail inmates are men. Women's incarceration rates have
increased more quickly than men's since 1980, but much
higher rates persist for men, leaving women to contend with
raising children while their partners cycle in and out of jail.
These men are young, of working age, many with small children. About two-thirds of state prisoners are over eighteen
years old but under age thirty-five. With this age pattern, only
a small number of people are incarcerated at any point in
time, but many more pass through the penal system at some
point in their lives. (Western & Wildeman, 2009, p. 228)

Western and Wildeman also noted that incarceration is highest among those
disadvantaged in terms of their socioeconomic status and years of schooling:

Incarceration is also concentrated among the disadvantaged.
High incarceration rates among low-status and minority
men are unmistakable. The 1997 survey of state and federal
prisoners shows that state inmates average less than eleven
years of schooling. A third were not working at the time of
their incarceration, and the average wage of the remainder
is much lower than that of other men with the same level of
education. African Americans and Hispanics also have
higher incarceration rates than whites, and together the two
groups account for about two-thirds of the state prison population. (p.228)

These same researchers also contend that there are differences in race/ethnic
group affiliations in the incarceration rates with Black men being more disproportionately represented in the criminal justice system as compared to
White men (2009, p.228).

Dr. Herron Keyon Gaston

The black-white difference in incarceration rates is especially striking. Black men are eight times more likely to be incarcerated than whites, and large racial disparities can be seen for all age groups and at different levels of education. The large black-white disparity in incarceration is unmatched by most other social indicators. Racial disparities in unemployment (two to one), nonmarital childbearing (three to one), infant mortality (two to one), and wealth (one to five) are all significantly lower than the eight to one black-white ratio in incarceration rates. If white men were incarcerated at the same rate as blacks, there would be more than 6 million people in prison and jail, and more than 5 percent of the male working-age population would be incarcerated (Western & Wildeman, 2009, p.228).

Further, Western and Wildeman (2009) also noted differences in concentrations of incarceration rates by age, race, and educational attainment.

Age, race, and educational disparities concentrate imprisonment among the disadvantaged. From 1980 to 2004, the percentage of young white men in prison or jail increased from 0.6 to 1.9 percent. Among young white men with only a high school education, incarceration rates were about twice as high. At the dawn of the prison boom, in 1980, the incarceration rate for young black men, 5.7 percent, was more than twice as high as that for low-education whites. By 2004, 13.5 percent of black men in their twenties were in prison or jail. Incarceration rates were higher in the lower half of the education distribution. More than one in five young noncollege black men were behind bars on a typical day in 2004 (Western & Wildeman, 2009, p.228).

These authors further contend that the impact that mass incarceration has on family life undercuts economic standing, the ability to model fatherhood to children, and ability to maintain positive and lasting relationships with significant others and children (Western & Wildeman, 2009, p.228).

Mass Incarceration and the Prison Industrial Complex: Unique Companions

The prison industrial complex (PIC) can be characterized best as the systematic enterprise of deep criminalization and expansive incarceration in scope, size, and negative outcomes within communities of color (Brewer & Heitzeg, 2008). The systematic practices of mass incarceration and over-crowding, imbedded in a "colorblind" ethos of criminal justice and public policy of reducing crime and maintaining social control, have created a large economic system of partnerships, facilities, and politics based on exploitation, greed, and free labor. Schlosser (1998) contended the following:

> Three decades after the war on crime began, the United States has developed a prison-industrial complex—a set of bureaucratic, political, and economic interests that encourage increased spending on imprisonment, regardless of the actual need. The prison-industrial complex is not a conspiracy, guiding the nation's criminal justice policy behind closed doors. It is a confluence of special interests that has given prison construction in the United States a seemingly unstoppable momentum. It is composed of politicians, both liberal and conservative, who have used the fear of crime to gain votes; impoverished rural areas where prisons have become a cornerstone of economic development; private companies that regard the roughly $35 billion spent each year on corrections not as a burden on American taxpayers but as a lucrative market; and government officials whose fiefdoms have expanded along with the inmate population. Since 1991 the rate of violent crime in the United States has fallen

by about 20 percent, while the number of people in prison
or jail has risen by 50 percent (p.304).

The relationship between the over criminalization of certain sectors of society, along with the lucrative and economic politicization of the prison and the criminal justice system as a capitalist industry, has created unique challenges for families, society, and the faith community. Therefore, mass incarnation in the United States seems to support the political goals of capitalism while ensuring a false sense of safety based on a socalled "color blind" system of justice.

These aspects taken together create possible dependence on the criminal justice system for socialization, skill development, education, and a prison family orientation. This long-term reliance and dependence on a system that strips identity, dehumanizes, and cripples potential opportunities for many offenders may lead to their inability to return to the community and reintegrate. This phenomenon of the "broken" person or spirit certainly can feed into the high rates of recidivism upon reentry into the community by many offenders (Biggs, 2009). This makes reentry quite a fearful and daunting task for the offender and those expecting their return.

Prison Reentry Defined

The Bureau of Justice Assistance (2012) defines prison reentry as the transition of offenders from prison to community supervision. This consists of those persons released from State or Federal prisons, or discharged from State parole, Federal parole, or Supervised release. How successful this transition will be depending on many factors prior to release and after release. The Urban Institute's Prisoner Reentry Portfolio (Solomon, Visher, LaVigne, & Osborne, 2006) focused on a variety of issues faced by ex-offenders retuning back to the community. The report noted that two-thirds of released prisoners will be arrested within three years of their release (Lanagan & Levin, 2002).

Further, securing and maintaining employment is an important factor in reentry success. Yet, research has shown that ex-offenders returning to the community face a plethora of issues such as low job skills, lack of education, transportation barriers, and the general reluctance of employers to hire ex-offenders (Solomon et al., 2006, p.4). Many of these issues can be further compounded with poor or no housing opportunities, substance use and abuse, lack of family support, and reluctant community social service support upon leaving the prison system (Solomon et al.2006).

Several studies have focused on reentry and many have focused on the problems associated with reentry success and adaptations versus failure and eventual return to prison (Hlavka, Wheelock & Jones, 2015; Solomon et al.2006). There has been an increase in interest around prison reentry of offenders and the contributions made by community supervision, family support, community support, and the faith community. As the political climate becomes more punitive in response to crime and those who commit crimes, a large population of people will not only be arrested but are likely to remain in prison for long periods of time.

A retrospective cohort study of 30,237 inmates released from the Washington State Department of Corrections from 1999-2003 found that released inmates were at greater risk for health issues and death (Binswanger et al., 2007). The study noted that 443 of the released inmates died during a mean follow-up period of 1.9 years. The study found that the overall mortality rate was 777 deaths per 1,000,000 persons each year. The adjusted death rate for released prisoners was 3.5 times that of other state residents. Interestingly, they found that during the first 2 weeks of release the risk of death was 12.7 times that of other residents. This same study found that the leading causes of death among those released were drug overdose, cardiovascular disease, homicide, and suicide (Binswanger et al, 2007).

These types of studies raise questions about the internal mechanisms that best prepare inmates for the outside life, and about those in the community who should be prepared to render assistance and support to this broken population. Prisoner reentry has raised concerns around public safety and how correctional systems should manage such individuals once they return to the community on supervision (Lynch & Sabol, 2001).

Recidivism: The Revolving Door Effect

Recidivism is considered a fundamental concept in criminal justice. Recidivism is used as a measure to determine the success of an offender's ability to reintegrate back into society and on some level the success of their rehabilitation while in prison (Lynch, 2014). Recidivism refers to a person's relapse into criminal behavior, often after the person receives sanctions or undergoes intervention for a previous crime. It represents the act of the person reverting, relapsing or repeating some behavior or the same crime behavior that landed them in jail or prison originally. Hence, the "revolving door" effect. While there are many factors associated with recidivism, we know that criminal history, criminal and health records, and other social demographic factors and environmental factors could impact rates of recidivism. In a recent special report from the Bureau of Justice Statistics on the recidivism of released prisoners in 30 states from 2005-2010, Durose, Cooper, and Snyder (2014) offered the following key highlights:

- About two-thirds (67.8%) of released prisoners were arrested for a new crime within 3 years, and three-quarters (76.6%) were arrested within 5 years.
- Within 5 years of release, 82.1% of property offenders were arrested for a new crime, compared to 76.9% of drug offenders, 73.6% of public order offenders, and 71.3% of violent offenders.
- More than a third (36.8%) of all prisoners who were arrested within 5 years of release were arrested within the first 6 months after release, with more than half (56.7%) arrested by the end of the first year.
- Two in five (42.3%) released prisoners were either not arrested or arrested once in the 5 years after their release.
- One sixth (16.1%) of released prisoners were responsible for almost half (48.4%) of the nearly 1.2 million arrests that occurred in the 5-year follow-up period.
- An estimated 10.9% of released prisoners were arrested in a state other than the one that released them during the 5-year follow-up period.

- Within 5 years of release, 84.1% of inmates who were age 24 or younger at release were arrested, compared to 78.6% of inmates ages 25 to 39 and 69.2% of those ages 40 or older.

A study of recidivism among 25,431 federal offenders with an eight-year followup found that almost half (49.3%) were rearrested for a new crime or rearrested for a violation of supervision conditions (United States Sentencing Commission, 2016). The study also found the following:

- Almost one-third (31.7%) of the offenders were also reconvicted, and one quarter (24.6%) of the offenders were reincarcerated over the same study period.
- Offenders released from incarceration in 2005 had a rearrests rate of 52.5%, while offenders released directly to a probationary sentence had a rearrests rate of 35.1%.
- Of those offenders who recidivated, most did so within the first two years of the eight-year follow-up period. The median time to rearrests was 21 months.
- About one-fourth of those rearrested had an assault rearrests as their most serious charge over the study period. Other most common serious offenses were drug trafficking, larceny, and public order offenses.
- A federal offender's criminal history was closely correlated with recidivism rates. Rearrests rates range from 30.2% for offenders with zero total criminal history points to 80.1% of offenders in the highest Criminal History Category, VI. Each additional criminal history point was generally associated with a greater likelihood of recidivism.
- A federal offender's age at time of release into the community was also closely associated with differences in recidivism rates. Offenders released prior to age 21 had the highest rearrests rate, 67.6%, while offenders over sixty years old at the time of release had a recidivism rate of

16.0%. Other factors, including offense type and educational level, were associated with differing rates of recidivism, but less so than age and criminal history.

As indicated, recidivism poses a great threat to successful reintegration of offenders back into the community and their families. The mass incarceration of thousands of Americans and the systematic practices of the prison industrial complex have fostered a broken segment of society with little hope for successful reintegration back into the community. Obviously more is needed from all sectors of society, particularly the faith community. Activities such as prison ministries have been instrumental in providing forgiveness, hope, and reconciliation from a Christian perspective, but more is needed once offenders return to their communities.

Prison Ministries: Internal and External

Prison ministries can take on many forms and provide a variety of spiritual, social, economic, and family support needs. Here, I wish to briefly distinguish between internal and external services. I define internal services as generally consisting of those ministries that take place while the offender is detained or in custody in one of the federal or state prisons and which are generally supervised or led by the Chaplaincy. A few examples of prison or internal ministries or chaplain focused programs are identified by the Center for Christian Ethics (2012).

Project TURN — Duke Divinity School students take in-prison classes beside their incarcerated brothers and sisters. The carefully selected readings, writing projects involving revision of multiple drafts, and open discussions invite all classmates to contribute fully from their varied backgrounds. The project's name TURN, an acronym for "Transform, Unlock, ReNew," was inspired by the Apostle Paul's teaching that we be transformed by the renewal of our minds as we are united to other members of Christ's Body (Romans 12:2-8; Center for Christian Ethics, 2012).

The Reading for Life — This program in St. Joseph County, IN, uses guided reflection on literature to nurture the moral imagination in juvenile offenders. Students meet with trained mentors to learn about classical and theological virtues, read some novels together, journal on relevant questions, and discuss the character implications in the readings and their writings. Then they plan and execute a related act of community service. By starting with the young people where they are, really listening to their life concerns, and having realistic expectations for their accomplishments, mentors seek to counter the dehumanization that juvenile offenders often experience in the justice system. Mentors see remarkable growth in students' skills and character (Center for Christian Ethics, 2012).

The Central Texas Hospitality House — Volunteers in Gatesville, TX provide an oasis of care for those who have traveled a great distance to visit a friend or family member incarcerated in one of the six state prisons in the town (Center for Christian Ethics, 2012).

External ministries would refer to those ministries in faith communities and churches that support the spiritual and social needs of the prisoner upon reentry back into the community. The literature has varied examples of internal and external ministries demonstrating their effectiveness in supporting the spiritual needs of the offender. In either case, whether internal or external, there is always some degree of risk and many programs have some type of religious, spiritual, or faith focus (Mears, Roman, Wolff, & Buck, 2006; Stansfield, Mowen, & O'Connor, 2017).

A wide range of faith-orientated reentry ministries are available to assist those who are reintegrating back into the community. Just as there are many internal types, there are just as many external faith oriented ministries to help offenders adjust, provide support, and reconnect to their families, jobs, housing, and education. A few examples are provided here to show the variety and complexity of those types of programs and the impetus for their development in the wake of mass incarceration for so many broken people who return from prison with little to no support and often end up returning to prison.

The American Baptist Churches USA, American Baptist Home Mission Societies (ABHMS) — The American Baptist Churches USA, American Baptist Home Mission Societies have a hallmark prisoner reentry program that is comprised of 20 members. The twenty-member team is comprised of local pastors, nonprofit leaders with backgrounds in reentry, lay leaders across the county, and prison chaplains across the

United States. These leaders have a keen interest in advancing the cause of reentry. Since 2007, the core mission of ABHMS (2007-18) is to make a transformational impact in communities most hit by the mass incarceration crisis. These leaders understand the importance of creating and fostering communities of hope by engaging, educating, and connecting with the community. The ethos of the organization is to inspire those who are impacted by mass incarceration to pick up the mantle in helping to articulate their own struggle, that would in turn, lead to concreate actions being taken to disarm such institutional inequality.

ABHMS has communities across the United States and Puerto Rico. The baseline of the organization is grounded in Christian principles, rooted in the idea of compassionate justice, and thereby seeking to be Christ's hands and feet to the world and being present to the communities to which they are called to serve. In addition, the

ABHMS understands the value of being connected to resources greater than themselves.

Therefore, they collaborate with churches outside of their connectional system but with similar aims towards eradicating inequality, using Christianity as a standard for forging more just and equitable communities. The terminology most associated with this form of collaboration is what the ABHMS organization describes as healing communities. The concept of healing communities was birthed following World War II in collaboration with Church World Service to address the issue of refugees being displaced. The organization boasts helping to assist more than 100,000 displaced persons from across the world, which included women, men, underserved children and families—and those from underrepresented populations in the urban center in the early 20th century.

Today, ABHMS continues to provide service to communities across the United States and Puerto Rico. In years past, ABHMS has sent volunteers to New Orleans to assist those devastated by Hurricane Katrina and other natural disasters since 2006. Other healing community initiatives that ABHMS has been involved in are: Ex-offender

Reentry, Justice for Children, Socially Responsible Investing and The Penny Project. ABHMS is dedicated to establishing a society that is more inclusive, compassionate, generous, and that ultimately promotes human flourishing by eradicating systemic and institutional injustice.

Presbyterian Church, USA — Three years ago, the Presbyterian Health Education and Welfare Association (PHEWA) convened a gathering of Presbyterians and members of other faith traditions (United Church of Christ, United Methodist Church and members of the Samuel Dewitt Proctor Conference) to develop a network that would address issues arising from our nation's criminal justice system. The result was the establishment of the Presbyterian Criminal Justice Network (PCJN). Its leadership ranges from individuals engaged in the struggle to abolish private prisons to those advocating an end to the death penalty and faith community leaders who have developed reentry programs for citizens returning to society after incarceration (Jones 2015). The network was formed at a time when the US criminal justice system was coming under increased scrutiny. From what the Children's Defense Fund calls the "cradle-to-prison pipeline" to mandatory sentencing for minor drug offenses, many people of faith, including Presbyterians, have concluded that the system is badly broken (Jones, 2015).

Many authors I consulted argue that the criminal justice system is more punitive than rehabilitative. Unless people have effective rehabilitative services, they will not be prepared to succeed when they return home. And it's no secret that persons of color are penalized disproportionately. The 'Resolution on Racism, Incarceration, and Restoration' was presented by the Advisory Committee on Racial Ethnic Concerns (ACREC) and approved by the 220th General Assembly in 2012).

United Methodist Church — The United Methodist Church has a long history of concern for social justice. Wesley and the early Methodists expressed their opposition to societal ills such as slavery, smuggling, inhumane prison conditions, alcohol abuse, and child labor. We believe that salvation entails renewal of both individuals and the world. Our faithful response to God's saving grace has both a personal and social dimension as we grow in "holiness of heart and life." By practicing spiritual disciplines, "works of piety," such as prayer, Bible study, and participation in corporate worship and communion, we grow and mature in our love for God. By engaging in acts of compassion and justice, "works of mercy" such as visiting the sick and those in prison, feeding the hungry, advocating for the poor and marginalized, we live out our love for God through service to our neighbor. According to the Book of Disciplines (United Methodist Church [UMC] 2012), "Our love of God is always linked with love of our neighbor, a passion for justice and renewal in the life of the world" (p. 51).

Just as our own discipleship occurs both at a personal and communal level, our work in the world extends beyond helping individuals to transforming the conditions that create injustice and inequality. "It is our conviction that the good news of the Kingdom must judge, redeem, and reform the sinful social structures of our time" (UMC, 2012, p.53). Our Social Principles are the church's prayerful and thoughtful attempt to speak to contemporary issues through a biblical and theological lens, seeking "to apply the Christian vision of righteousness to social, economic, and political issues" (UMC, p.53). As the agency tasked specifically to assist The United Methodist Church's work of advocacy, The United Methodist Board of Church and Society works to provide "witness and action on issues of human well-being, justice, peace" through research, education and training.

The Role of Religion and Faith on Desistance from Crime

Christian communities have been on the forefront of prison ministries and prison reentry and issues related to forgiveness, support assistance, prevention, intervention, and even reducing further criminal acts and recidivism (Stansfield, Mowen, & O'Connor, 2017). Stansfield et al. (2017) have also explored research in the area of religion and desistance to determine the effects of such interactions on lower future offending or recidivism. The ability of churches, and the power of religious systems, to organize, integrate, and sustain a community is still a valuable concept and framework to determine whether this association with the faith community has efficacy in reducing or preventing crime. The establishment and requirement of trust in religious principle, or identification with a higher power are inherent in most religious systems and faith communities. Several researchers have found these and other components to be essential to the success of reentry while in prison and outside of prison.

Although there are numerous reasons one may choose to participate in religious programming, or seek support from religious leaders and organizations, four in every five state prison chaplains consider the support obtained from religious groups after release to be "absolutely critical" to successful reentry in society (Pew Forum, 2009; Pew Research Center, 2012; Roberts & Stacer, 2016; Schroeder & Frana, 2009; Stansfield et al., 2017).

Summary

This chapter sought to provide an understanding of the nature and complexity of mass incarceration, the prison industrial complex in America, and the problems associated with this burgeoning population for humanity and especially for the church. A special focus on the impact and problem of recidivism as a result of this epidemic was also explored. Support for prison ministries and for those reentering the community were explored along with examples of those faith communities who have already explored and are actively involved in prison ministry and fostering a community of care at release.

CHAPTER THREE

The Church Response to Prison Reentry

Introduction

The purpose of this chapter is to provide insight into the role of the Church in general in prison reentry as part of the expected mission of the Church in the wake of the growing epidemic of mass incarceration and criminalization of certain subgroups of people and how this impact has created a large number of people who are more likely to experience barriers and other difficulties being reintegrated back into the community. Explored are issues related to recidivism and desistance, or cessation, of crime. An integrated conversation about the role of the United Methodist Church and its historical relevance in assisting as a reformer, redeemer, and reformer is supported from its Wesleyan tradition.

The Role of the Church in Prison Reentry

The Church can play a pivotal role in prison reentry for a variety of reasons. The Church has a long history of support to individuals, families, and communities and has provided health care, clothing, food, and shelter to those in need. Life after prison can be challenging and daunting. Discrimination, marginalization, and even racial profiling can impact how well someone might be reintegrated back into the community (Hansen, 2015). The most critical time after release is the first month. Hansen noted the following issues that can confront those returning to the community after prison.

> The Church can play a critical role in receiving recently released citizens back into their communities. Indeed, we are called to "let mutual love continue. Do not neglect to show hospitality to strangers, for by doing that some have entertained angels without knowing it. Remember those who are in prison, as though you were in prison with them; those who are being tortured, as though you yourselves were being tortured" (Hebrews 13:1-3). Jesus himself was put on trial, found guilty, imprisoned, placed on death row, and ultimately subject to capital punishment by the state. If we are to identify with Christ, we are to identify with those who find themselves in similar situations today. (para 6)

I would argue that local churches can play a major role in the transformation of returning citizens. First, churches must be intentional in our mission and our prayers for restoration and renewal of incarcerated persons. The Church must then go outside its walls and into the highways, byways and local prisons and invite people to come into the church[2]. Churches must pray and encourage those about to be released back into the community, and must not judge people based on their perceivable indiscretions. Churches must walk intentionally with people through the process of being reoriented back in the community, and must pray for the systems of injustice and their many representatives to be more just and equitable, thus promoting human flourishing instead engaging in the degradation of humanitarian compassion.

In addition, churches must extend radical hospitality in the truest sense of the word. It is not enough to pray for formerly incarcerated individuals and leave the prayers at the altar. Rather, formerly incarcerated persons must feel included in the worship community. Therefore, I would propose that churches incorporate into their structure "prayers for the people" that would

---

[2] The guiding principle for going outside our church walls comes from Luke 14:23.

Dr. Herron Keyon Gaston

reflect Matthew 25:36 in that: "I needed clothes and you clothed me, I was sick and you looked after me, I was in prison and you came to visit me." With this verse included explicitly, it would demonstrate churches' intention to address the issue of mass incarceration and their commitment to the restorative justice process.

Ideally, as prayers are being lifted for formerly incarcerated individuals, the idea would be to forge communities of compassion that would serve as a vehicle through which people come together in dialogue to share and witness the transformational power of the Holy Spirit through testimonials and the extending of shared resources. This in turn, hopefully, will organically move into Bible study sessions and educational enlightenment around mass incarceration and the prison industrial complex.

Next, churches in partnership with local correctional institutions, should serve as bridge builders between inmates and the community. Inmates who are about to be released within a specific period of time should cultivate relationships with local churches, so as to make the transition back into the community smoother. Churches could accomplish this goal by sending birthday, Thanksgiving, and Christmas cards to this targeted population. Next, the members of the congregation during a designated time in the church service, could sign the cards individually as a collective enterprise on behalf of the church. Churches that are anchored in local municipalities should work with local governmental officials to declare local cities and sanctuaries as "sanctuary communities," which serves to protect and safeguard the interest of the formerly incarcerated community. According to Hansen (2015),

> It is important to engage your congregation early and often around these issues to help increase awareness and compassion. Similarly, it is important that the entire worshiping community remain mindful and prayerful together, not simply leaving it as a specialized interest of a few. Lift up the prisons and those ministering with them as a community, knowing that you are responding to God's call to remember the incarcerated (para. 2).

While engaging in this work, one could anticipate some pushback and moments of frustration. The multilayered bureaucracy associated with prison ministry is daunting and can seem insurmountable. Every community context is different and the challenges around this work are nuanced and complex. Navigating the system with positive impact can bring the best out of us — and it can also bring the worse out of us in terms of challenging the particular social context through which we interpret the role and actions of the work. Hansen would assert, "we learn many things about ourselves and our own culture's assumptions and values when we encounter those different from ourselves. And it is in so doing that we see the face of God."

Johnson (2008) recognized in his research the important and vital role that faith communities and churches play in prison reentry though the tough transition process. He recognized the impact of prison systems on the humanity of humans since the dawn of time. Yet, in either case, prisoners have expressed difficulty in the integrative and transition process. Johnson feels that the major issue is the sheer number of those who will be retuning back to communities with limited knowledge, education, resources, and, to some degree, as broken individuals. Therefore, he points out the following dilemmas for returning prisoners:

> As long as prisons have existed, prisoners have had difficulty in transitioning back into society. In the United States, the process of reintegrating ex-prisoners into society has been a problem in need of a solution for many decades. What is different now is the sheer number of prisoners returning to American communities each year. What has been referred to as an unprecedented and disturbing development is now beginning to be recognized for what it is not: a temporary trend. Between 1980 and 2006, the U.S. prison population increased by 467 percent (from 319,598 to 1,492,973), and the parole population increased by 362 percent (from 220,438 to 798,202) (Johnson, 2008, p.3; U.S. Department of Justice 2006). The inevitable increase in the number of prisoners returning to communities across

the country has created a national debate about how best to handle what has become known as the prisoner reentry crisis, one of the most challenging dilemmas in correctional history. (Johnson, 2008, p.3).

Johnson (2008) also noted the stark statistical reality of the problems faced by prisoners after leaving prison and the reality of multiple rearrests:

A number of well-known correctional programs have been implemented over the years to help manage the difficult adjustment period when prisoners transition back into society. Halfway houses, community corrections, intensive supervision, and community reintegration programs represent but a few of the various postrelease efforts designed to make prisoner reentry into society less difficult for exprisoners while ensuring public safety. But despite corrections expenditures that are now in excess of $60 billion annually, the likelihood that a former prisoner will succeed in the community has not improved. Indeed, about two thirds of all offenders who leave prison are rearrested within three years of their release. Growing caseloads have made effective case management by parole officers increasingly difficult. A byproduct is increasing occupational stress on parole officers. As a result of these conditions, there is increasing concern that the number of exprisoners returning to society could pose a major threat to public safety. Even though the problems faced by ex-prisoners returning to society are readily identifiable, public efforts to address these reentry and aftercare problems have been limited (Johnson, 2008, p.3).

The Role of the Church in Prison Reentry: The Good and the Bad

Johnson (2008) noted that the faith-based prisoner reentry programming or model has a variety of shortcomings. At the same time, this model contains some hopeful components for future potential success. He noted the following:

> As important as volunteer work within correctional facilities might be, it does not diminish the fact that reentry and aftercare tend to be largely overlooked by most religious volunteers and organizations. Compared to reentry, prison ministry is a much easier task to pursue and a safe service opportunity in what many consider to be an unsafe environment. Prisoners often appreciate the attention they receive from the outside world, and these exchanges tend to be overwhelmingly positive and nonthreatening for volunteers. Prison ministry, therefore, can be found in many U.S. congregations and among the thousands of religious volunteers who visit prisons every day. Likewise, faith-based organizations disproportionately opt for in-prison ministry rather than out-of-prison services because reentry and aftercare are anything but easy or safe. For example, Prison Fellowship Ministries (PF), the largest faith-based prison ministry in the United States, has always recognized that reentry and aftercare are vitally important, but PF's efforts have been only marginally involved in these areas. This oversight was recently acknowledged by PF president Mark Early, at a White House "Compassion in Action" Roundtable event on prisoner reentry in March 2007, when he stated an intention to remedy the imbalance by significantly expanding the organization's aftercare emphasis. While the disproportionate emphasis on volunteerism is in prisons rather than on aftercare in communities is undeniable, it would be inaccurate to suggest that faith-based prisoner reentry programs are nonexistent. Unfortunately, it is unclear how many faith-based reentry programs are in operation, though it is likely that they exist in many of the communities where prisons are located. Faith-based prisoner reentry programs tend to be

small, isolated, and in need of coordination as well as evaluation (Johnson, 2008, p.7).

Nonetheless, churches have a unique ability to invest in the humanity of reentering prisoners and help to restore dignity, purpose, and will. The spiritual connectivity that occurs probably cannot be absolutely measured. However, we know something meaningful and transformative is taking place when many offenders engage in such programs at the community level.

The United Methodist Church: Historical Overview

The United Methodist Church has its earliest roots in the Wesleyan tradition, roots connected to the lives and ministries of John Wesley (1703-1791) and his brother Charles Wesley (1707-1788). The early Methodist church was based on the Church of England and they served as priests and volunteered as missionaries in the New World Colony of Georgia in 1736 (United Methodist Church, 2012). Methodism began to emerge in America from 1770-1816 with authorization and support from England as other lay immigrants came to America.

Currently, the United Methodist Church in the United States has a total church jurisdictional membership of 7,067,162, with 32,148 active churches, 47,271 clergy members, and an average weekly worship attendance of 2,749,926, 56 annual conferences, 46 episcopal areas, and 5 jurisdictions. (United Methodist Church, 2015).

The United Methodist Church and Social Justice Ministries

To help guide its moral and ethical obligations, the United Methodist Church (2012) established its *Book of Disciplines: General Rules and Social Principles*. The Social Principles provide the framework and ethos of the United Methodist Church around righteousness on social, economic, and political issues. They convey the guidelines, disposition, and discipline of its members and the life of the church. The United Methodist church is very deliberate and careful to note that *"a church that rushes to punishment is not open to God's mercy, but a church lacking the courage to act decisively on personal and social issues loses its claim to moral authority. The church exercises its discipline as a community though which God continues to reconcile the world to himself"* (p.27).

The United Methodist Church believes that the good news of the Kingdom must judge, redeem, and reform the sinful social structures of our time. Thus, this denomination is structured and posed ethically and morally to carry out the work of those who have been taken away from God though sin, crime, or other vice; and the United Methodist Church has a duty to proclaim and demand social justice while restoring the wounded back to God.

The people of the United Methodist Church have common Christian roots: God, Jesus, The Holy Spirit, Human Beings, the Church, the Bible, and the belief that God reigns in all as a present reality and as hope for the future. Thus, the Social Creed of the United Methodist Church states:

> Our "Social Creed" is a basic statement of our convictions about the fundamental relationships between God, God's creation, and humanity. This basic statement is expanded in a lengthier statement called the "Social Principles." This statement explains more fully how United Methodists are called to live in the world. Part of our *Book of Discipline*, the "Social Principles" serve as a guide to official church action and our individual witness (United Methodist Church 2012, p.92 Para 4).

United Methodist Church
Mission Plan for Restorative Justice Ministries

The Mission Plan for Restorative Justice Ministries (2004) was established based on the Social Principles and the creed of the United Methodist Church throughout the world as a call to the church to engage actively in ministries supporting the broken and the wayward. Adopted in 2004 by the United Methodist Church, this plan reflects the sense of readiness of the United

Methodist Church not only to continue to engage more deeply in the prison reentry, but also to empower all peoples of the United Methodist Church to engage more directly in both internal and external ministries of the prison and detained populations. The United Methodist Church recognizes the current justice system as a retributive system which in many ways hurts the victims, the offenders, and the community. Further, the Mission Plan reflects the vision for restorative justice for the United Methodist Church and provides an initial call to action wherein change can be seen and made thought its connectional church structure via the general church level, the specific general church agencies, the jurisdictional/central conference and annual conference levels, and at the local level.

It is my hope that this project and dissertation can serve as a catalyst for a more detailed blueprint and action plan for the United Methodist Church, grounded in social justice, redemptive spirit, and wholeness of the person. The proposed action plan can strengthen and empower UMC congregations around the world to assist those in prison and to support and prepare them for reentry and reintegration back into the community. Further, these elements of social justice, redemptive spirit, and wholeness are imbedded in the mission of the United Methodist Church as a reformer, redeemer, and restorer community. Consequently, the ideas and motives of the United Methodist Church positions the Church to be able to understand and take on the mission of prison reentry. This call to action creates the foundation for a blueprint for justice throughout the United Methodist Church system.

United Methodist Church as Reformer, Redeemer, and Restorer: "Open Hearts, Open Minds, Open Doors"

UMC as a Reformer

Since the beginning of the United Methodist Church's faith tradition, the UMC was to be seen as a reforming institution. Within the framework of the Wesley brothers' teachings and vision, the UMC would be altered from the traditional and historical Methodist tradition in England as a movement that sought to change the theological system through sermons, theological treatises, journals, letters, diaries, hymns, and other spiritual writings. Therefore, Wesleyanism as it was expanded to the Georgia colonies in the New World would focus more on personal faith, personal experiences, and holiness. The love of God was to be supreme and one was to love God totally and completely with one's heart, soul, mind, and strength. Further, one was to love one's neighbors as they loved themselves. Even more importantly, this new system stressed the experiential religion and moral responsibility that its parishioners should endeavor to espouse. Therefore, God's love was to be of supreme importance and since we are created in God's image, we must make every effort to seek and establish justification by faith as a pathway to sanctification or scriptural holiness (UMC, 2012).

As noted in Article XII of the church's Articles of Religion, the following can help us understand the role of forgiveness as our duty in the Methodist tradition:

> Not every sin willingly committed after justification is the sin against the Holy Ghost, and unpardonable. Wherefore, the grant of repentance is not to be denied to such as fall into sin after justification. After we have received the Holy Ghost, we may depart from grace given, and fall into sin, and, by the grace of God, rise again and amend our lives. And therefore, they are to be condemned who say they can no more sin as long as they live here; or deny the place of forgiveness to such as truly repent (UMC, 2012, p.23)

Wesley established the connection as a way of moving closer to God. Further, this connection between sanctification and the relationship with God was to be a component of one's mind and one's heart, from which great and Godly work would be inspired and seen for all to witness. This idea makes the Wesleyan tradition and United Methodist Church more than a reforming institution of change from the English tradition as it was transformed in the New World and especially in the original Georgia Colony. The notion of the United Methodist Church as a reformer can take on a double meaning.

First, the United Methodist Church itself has been changed in fundamental theological and doctrinal ways to move closer to God and understand that the sources of authority such as: scripture, reason, tradition, and experience must all be understood within the context of grace as an internal and external source of God's work, and through the scriptural teachings. It must be understood here that we are made in the image of God and God came to make us whole and fulfill all good things and not to destroy humanity. Therefore, we must work to restore this perfect image of God through all that we believe and do on earth. This includes our personal and faith commitment to those who may have fallen, sinned, or in some way transgressed the way in which God wishes us to live.

Article VII of the United Methodist Church regarding Original or Birth Sin and Article VII: Of Free Will, situates humankind in the following manner:

> Original sin standeth not in the following of Adam (as the Pelagians do vainly talk), but it is the corruption of the nature of every man, that naturally is engendered of the offspring of Adam, whereby man is very far gone from original righteousness, and of his own nature inclined to evil, and that continually (UMC, 2012, p.13).

Regarding "Free Will," Article VII reads:

> The condition of man after the fall of Adam is such that he cannot turn and prepare himself, by his own natural strength and works, to faith, and calling upon God; wherefore we have no power to do good works, pleasant and acceptable to God, without the grace of God by Christ preventing us, that we may have a good will, and working with us, when we have that good will (UMC, 2012).

This includes our institutional commitment to atrocities and crippling role of the criminal justice system on our society. We must seek to assist in reforming this punitive and life altering system. Those of the United Methodist Church and the Wesleyan tradition do not have the luxury of sitting on the side lines while humanity is being destroyed. All of us are created in His image and therefore we must be proactive in changing this system of oppression and retribution.

Second, because of this Wesleyan tradition, the United Methodist Church member or leader has a personal, spiritual, and Godly duty to carry out their role as a reforming agent. Thus, each member and leader within the United Methodist Church within the Wesleyan tradition must make every effort under the authority of the church to help those who have been broken receive the opportunity to seek the goodness and grace of God and set them on a path to redemption, and restoration as a new image in God. The assurance doctrine allows for us to know that anyone can be forgiven and saved through the Holy Spirit and grace.

UMC as a Redeemer

Through the grace of God and the redeeming qualities of grace and assurance, a person who has sinned or transgressed can be redeemed back into the fold of the believers and begin to be accepted and do good works before God and the community. Redemption can be defined as deliverance from death literally or figuratively by means of payment of a very high price (Schroeder, 2005). Many prisoners who return back to their communities find the doors closed with no one willing to purchase them back.

However, given the tradition and faith of the United Methodist Church, no one who seeks God should be turned away. Nor should we wait for those who have been broken to come to us, we must be missionaries as were the Wesley brothers and others that spurred this movement in the 1700s and until the present time. Therefore, we must be prepared to work within the confines of the United Methodist Church. Article X: Of Good Works helps us to understand what is pleasing and acceptable to God. The actions described must not be done for show or any other selfish or vain act.

> Although good works, which are the fruits of faith, and follow after justification, cannot put away our sins, and endure the severity of God's judgment; yet are they pleasing and acceptable to God in Christ, and spring out of a true and lively faith, insomuch that by them a lively faith may

be as evidently known as a tree is discerned by its fruit (UMC, 2012, p.39).

Sin can be characterized as a symbol of Satan or evil spirits, or other divisive elements in our nature. God's redeeming abilities can be best illustrated in the United Methodist tradition as Jesus Christ's death and the blood he shed for our sins and therefore we were made free or redeemed for we are purchased with a price. Several scriptures of the New Testament characterize this redemptive quality and the Methodist church believes that the scriptures make up one of the four theological authorities of the church. Additionally, the desire of all members who join the United Methodist Church must commit to the following membership duties in respect to dealing with others:

> To do good as much as is possible to all people as God gives opportunity, especially to those in the body of Christ; by giving food to the hungry, by clothing the destitute, by visiting or helping those who are sick or in prison; by instructing, correcting or encouraging them in love. (Matt 25:31–46; Eph 5:11; 1 Thess 5:14; Heb 3:13; 10:23–25)

One must recognize that that there are different levels of redemption. Nonetheless, we recognize here that God's grace and the power of the Holy Spirit allow us to be delivered from or brought back from some state of oppression, unrest, or ungodly state to be redeemed and renewed in the spirit of God and among other believers of the faith. Redemption is being on the road to salvation. When one returns back to the community, we expect the United Methodist Church to be a source of reformation given the past of the prisoner. We also expect the United Methodist Church to assist in the redemption and deliverance of persons from their former adversary and kidnapper, the criminal justice system, to restore them back to God.

UMC as a Restorer

The character and mission of the United Methodist Church and the Wesleyan tradition also position the church through God's authority to restore anyone who has fallen from grace, the church, and from the acceptable ways of Christian life to be reconnected and reengaged in a fashion that brings them back to God in sprit and in love. This vast power of God's authority seeks to bring all of humanity under God's divine care in preparation for Christ's coming through the substance of Christ's resurrection, the Holy Ghost, and Scriptures of Salvation. Article V of the Articles of Religion of the Methodist Church states:

> The Holy Scripture containeth all things necessary to salvation; so that whatsoever is not read therein, nor may be proved thereby, is not to be required of any man that it should be believed as an article of faith, or be thought requisite or necessary to salvation. In the name of the Holy Scripture we do understand those canonical books of the Old and New Testament of whose authority was never any doubt in the church. (UMC, 2012, p.40)

Above all, the United Methodist Church believes that God's purpose for humanity comes with a clear requirement to love the Lord and our neighbors as ourselves with all our hearts. This can be best summarized in the Articles of Religion of the Methodist Church:

> We believe that the two great commandments which require us to love the Lord our God with all the heart, and our neighbors as ourselves, summarize the divine law as it is revealed in the Scriptures. They are the perfect measure and norm of human duty, both for the ordering and directing of families and nations, and all other social bodies, and for individual acts, by which we are required to acknowledge God as our only Supreme Ruler, and all persons as created by Him, equal in all-natural rights. Therefore, all persons should so order all their individual, social and political acts as to give to God entire and absolute obedience, and to assure to all the enjoyment of every natural right, as well as to

promote the fulfillment of each in the possession and exercise of such rights. (UMC, 2012, p.220)

Consequently, this means that not only does the United Methodist Church as an institution have an obligation to help to restore humanity, but individual members have a duty to do likewise. Consequently, the United Methodist Church believes and compels us to seek love as a main ingredient that will allow us to love the criminal or ex-offender as our own neighbor and friend in Christ and seek to restore them back to God for our final calling. The reforming, redemptive, and restorative qualities and characteristics of the United Methodist Church are all important forces in helping to create a safe place for prison reentry back into the community, but more importantly, to restore them back to God such that their lives and mission can be forever changed. These three fundamental elements support the dimensions and power of liberation, hope, and justice as presented by Pounder (2008) and the tenets of restitution, accountability, forgiveness, personal responsibility, worthiness/redemption, discipline, fairness, and reconciliation of restorative justice (Garlitz, 1993). However, the greatest of all of these is love as characterized in the United Methodist Church and illustrated though scripture. These must be at the foundation for true reformation, redemption, and restoration of ourselves and those who seek our support and guidance upon reentry back to the community following imprisonment.

Summary

This chapter sought to explore and understand the Church's response to the problem and impact of mass incarceration, the prison industrial complex and high rates of recidivism, and the role of the church in liberating and supporting those who have been negatively impacted by the criminal justice system. Doctrinal and theological views about the social justice ministries within the United Methodist Church were highlighted with a special focus on the United Methodist Church as a reformer, redeemer, and the as a restorer in this effort of prison reentry and as part of their foundational mandate.

CHAPTER FOUR

The Summerfield United Methodist Church
Prison Reentry Model

Introduction

In this chapter, I will share the development of the prison reentry ministry that the Summerfield United Methodist Church has been blessed to offer to the community. As part of this program overview, I will share the history of Summerfield's founding, the focus on building an inclusive community, the specific actions we address, and the seven core areas of recovery we implement. I will also share a series of testimonials written by participants in the Summerfield program. These testimonials demonstrate the beauty of human vulnerability, as well as tell the story of Summerfield's intervention in changing lives and recovering souls for God.

The research, reports and statistics presented in this chapter are unpublished data, collected by Summerfield UMC through ongoing tracking and focus groups to evaluate our reentry ministry and programs for formerly incarcerated persons. We have made our program results available to the larger UMC community, as well as other denominations, primarily in inner cities and serving hard-to-reach populations, including the economically and racially disadvantaged.

A Brief Historical Overview
and Context for Mission Work and Outreach

Summerfield United Methodist Church in Bridgeport, Connecticut is an off-shoot of Park Methodist Episcopal Church. On January 1, 1871, the Rev. W.W. Bowish, the then pastor of Park Methodist Episcopal Church met with a group of clergymen to organize a Methodist Society on the east side of Bridgeport. The intention of this meeting was to discuss the vision of creating a new ministry. A group of clergypersons met on Barnum Avenue at an undisclosed location, thought to have been a vacant appliance store, to discuss the church's future at Summerfield's current location at Clermont Avenue in Bridgeport, on the corner of Ridgefield Avenue and Judson Street.

At the time of the meeting, Pastor Parkington was studying for ministry at a seminary in New York City. On January 15, 1871, Pastor Parkington delivered his initial sermon to a group of clergypersons in Bridgeport. After the delivery of his first sermon, people all across Bridgeport wanted to hear his inspirational messages. The church which would later be called Summerfield United Methodist Church, started with thirty members and the congregation grew exponentially over the next five years.

On February 19, 1872, the Methodist Society officially bore the name Summerfield United Methodist Episcopal Church. The church was named after a famous circuit rider, John Summerfield. The church quickly began the search process to name a new pastor. However, the process ended abruptly when the members of the congregation unanimously voted to name Pastor Parkington as their desired pastor. As a consequence of this request, Mr. Parkington was appointed the first pastor. In 1914, Summerfield United Methodist Church and the parsonage in both their current forms were constructed. The entire project was completed between 1922-1923.

Twenty-nine years after the full construction of the church, the church would merge with Grant Street German Church. The church added another 200 plus members as a result of this partnership. Summerfield also received new members from the Newfield Church, a church ministry that merged with another United Methodist Church in Bridgeport, Golden Hill UMC. Summerfield is known for its radical inclusion of people from all walks of life, demographics, and socioeconomic backgrounds.

Summerfield United Methodist Church is the "Light on the Hill" in Bridgeport and has been for more than 148 years. It is one of only two United Methodist Churches remaining in the City of Bridgeport. Summerfield continues to serve as a place of refuge for those seeking the radical love of Christ. Summerfield's ministry has grown tremendously over the years, and its ministries are a vital part of the Bridgeport community.

Adoption of Prison Fellowship Ministry

In 2002, Summerfield United Methodist Church adopted a prison fellowship ministry geared towards assisting formerly incarcerated individuals and helping them to reintegrate back into society. This unique ministry within Summerfield consists of members, laity, volunteers, and sister organizations and congregations within the greater Fairfield County area of Bridgeport. We focus squarely on advocacy, connecting individuals to resources within the community, and empowering individuals to become advocates for themselves. The volunteers, lay people, pastors of SUMC, along with other stakeholders in the community gather every fourth and fifth Sunday at 1pm for a separate service devoted specifically to this population.

Since 2015, our prison ministry has expanded tremendously under my leadership as Senior Pastor. We have expanded our outreach efforts across the City of Bridgeport and into New Haven County. I have created and led "compassion" ministry that focuses on the immediate needs of ex-offenders, their families, and their victims. We work very closely with the Bridgeport Police Department, the Bridgeport Mayor's Office, as well as other policymakers and parole boards in helping released prisoners to make a smooth transition back into the community. Our prison fellowship program is tasked with planning and conducting worship services and programs throughout the State of Connecticut.

We work closely with local, state, and national policymakers on common sense legislation reform around prison reentry initiatives. We encourage our laity – through our "compassionate eyes" ministry to correspond with prisoners by way of establishing a pen pal relationship. We provide this population with educational/vocational material, which aims to assist them in finding job opportunities. We collect gifts for the holidays and distribute gifts to prisoners' families on their behalf as a way to keep families connected. We also work with the Connecticut Assembly and the Criminal Justice Appropriations Committee on best practices in the area of faith-based best practices, and provide inspiration and outreach to other faith-based communities interested in establishing their own prison outreach programs.

Summerfield's Vision Statement and Commitment to Prison Fellowship Ministry

Summerfield United Methodist Church is dedicated to establishing an atmosphere in which every person who walks through our doors feels respected, valued, and part of our beloved community. Our Prison Fellowship program seeks to reintegrate/restore people back to their families, their communities, and ultimately back to God. We believe that social justice is at the heart of the Christian gospel and that we have a biblical mandate to extend Christ's eschatological hope to all of humanity, but especially those who have been marginalized by society. Our goal is to create compassionate, forgiving, and healing communities that focus on bringing prisoners, victims, and their families to new levels of compassion that can be experienced through God's grace.

We seek to educate wardens, prison personnel, volunteers, police departments, parole boards, advocates, and other humanitarian justice-seekers in ways in which we can create God's beloved community here on earth where we all coexist and feel valued as fellow human being reconciled through Christ. We advocate for smart policies around criminal justice reform and work with local police departments in helping to create safer communities where the aim is to transform prisoners into productive and contributing members of society. We advocate for restorative values, and we are dedicated to character development, relying on biblical texts to help transform one from the inside out. We partner with other organizations and churches in the community to support families, children, victims, and inmates on ways to improve their own lives and the life of their community. Below I will give details into the programs we offer at Summerfield United Methodist Church in conjunction with our Prison Fellowship Program. Moreover, you will find bullet points outlining our services, providing pertinent background information into the issue before outlining our actual program. The program is structured to:

- Connect ex-offenders with drug/rehabilitation treatment programs.
- Provide a temporary (30 day) emergency shelter for those released from prison within the last 30 days. We have 22 individual beds.
- Create healing communities, where we bring certified counselors to work closely with ex-offenders in processing their past and envisioning a better/new future.
- Connect ex-offenders with jobs/employers in the community.
- Connect ex-offenders with educational opportunities and walk them through the difficult college admissions process.
- Work closely with Residential Alcohol Treatment Facilities / and Drug Rehab organizations.
- Provide Section 8 assistance in helping to get ex-offenders placed into permanent housing.
- Work with the Department of Motor Vehicles to get people registered to drive so that they can get to and from work.
- Host trainings/workshops whereby ex-offenders are able to receive soft-skill training that can provide them with transferable skills into the workforce (i.e. internet training, social media engagement, interviewing skills/techniques).

Understanding the Issue, Unpacking the Problem:
In 1974 at the beginning of the era now known as Mass Incarceration, Robert Martinson wrote an article "What Works? Questions and Answers about Prison Reform." In this article, Martinson (1974) set out to look at the literature on prison rehabilitative treatments and answer the question of what works. He concluded that our prison system's focus on rehabilitation is not working and that society should focus more on deterrence strategies to prevent future crime. Since Martinson's article, the U.S. prison system has undergone changes in terms of moving from the penitentiary model to the correctional model. The under-

lying philosophy is that there is human value and potential that given the right conditions can lead to crime-free lives upon release where people can become productive members of society. Yes, there is still a punishment element in the new correctional model, but punishment is not the end goal – rehabilitation is.

Therefore, if we were to ask what works today, we would have to look at present programming in prison and find a metric to judge its success. The standard by which to judge can be found in the mission statements of any state's correctional institutions. For example, New York State's Department of Corrections has this as its vision and mission statement:

> Enhance public safety by having incarcerated persons return home under supportive supervision less likely to revert to criminal behavior.

> To improve public safety by providing a continuity of appropriate treatment services in safe and secure facilities where offenders' needs are addressed and they are prepared for release, followed by supportive services under community supervision to facilitate a successful completion of their sentence.

Connecticut offers a similar articulation. A five-year study compiled in 2012 by the State Criminal Policy and Planning Division of the Office of Policy Management found 79% of those released from Connecticut prisons were rearrested within 5 years with 69% convicted of a new crime. This study shows Connecticut's recidivism rate is significantly higher than the national average of approximately 66%[3]. Research further indicates that in Connecticut, nearly 50% of both the prison and jail population derives from only a few neighborhoods in five cities, which have the highest levels of concentrated poverty and minority populations in the state[4]. The City of Bridgeport is one of these five cities, and

---

[3] State of Connecticut Department of Corrections. *Recidivism*. Available at http://www.ct.gov/doc/cwp/view.asp?a=1492&Q=305970&docNav=l. See also Office of Policy and Management. 2011 *Annual Connecticut Recidivism Report*. Available at http://www.ct.gov/opm/cwp/view.asp?a=2976&Q= 383710&opmNav_GID=1797&opmNav=l466

[4] Council of State Governments, *Building Bridges: From Conviction to Employment, A Proposal to Reinvest Corrections Savings in an Employment Initiative*, January 2003. Available at: www.csgeast. org/crimpub.asp.

the East end section, where Summerfield provides services, constitutes the area with the highest percentage of prison admissions per capita in the entire city[5]. Summerfield offers individualized case management services and a supportive sober-house living environment, we have come to understand research shows are [5]critical to long-term successful reintegration into the community[6].

Bard Prison Initiative (BPI) Executive Director Max Kenner, in an interview on Democracy Now, noted that approximately 98% of the people who graduate from BPI do not return to prison[7]. In other words, the recidivism rate for BPI graduates is less than 2%. Compare this to the 79% recidivism rate in Connecticut and the 50% recidivism rate in New York and we have to ask the question how much of an interest do our State officials have in the debate about incarceration: who gets what, when, where and how?

Therefore, programs such as the one that is offered at Summerfield are critically important to the successful integration of formerly incarcerated individuals. Based on the data produced by Summerfield United Methodist Church, our prison Fellowship Program places more than 90% of formerly incarcerated individuals into colleges and universities, and has a 95% success rate in helping to put people into the workforce. So far, less than 1% of formerly incarcerated individuals we serve reoffended. This means that our program is just as effective as the program that Bard College touts. Although our church does this on a much smaller scale, we are extremely effective. In 2015 we adopted 7 key principles, named below, as being the driving force behind our success in the City of Bridgeport.

Commitment to Connecting
Formerly Incarcerated Individuals to Community Resources
At Summerfield we think that it is mission critical to pool the community's resources together and to take seriously the great needs of those we seek to serve. We understand that although we have a strong foothold in the greater

[5] Justice Mapping Center. *New Haven Analysis* – Jan. 2006. Available at http://www.justicemapping.org/#.

[6] Urban Institute. Understanding The Challenges Of Prisoner Reentry, 2006. Available at http://www.urban.org/research/publication/understanding-challenges-prisonerreentry/view/full_report.

[7] Resolved: Debate Win for Inmates Against Harvard Shows Benefits of Higher Education Behind Bars, Democracynow.org

Bridgeport community, it is crucially important to our success to collaborate with other social justice and faith based organizations to address the holistic concerns of formerly incarcerated individuals.

In addition, we believe that through biblically based programs and our restorative justice pilot initiative, we can help individuals who (perhaps once) broke the law to be transformed and mobilized to help strengthen their own communities, their neighbors, and serve as model citizens of society. But more importantly, through their commitment to public service, they will bear witness to the Gospel by serving others and living out the tenets of the Corporal Works of Mercy. At Summerfield, we believe that no life is beyond God's redemptive power, and we envision a future where formerly incarcerated persons and their families are reconciled, redeemed, and restored back to society by the unyielding compassion and love of Jesus Christ. We endeavor to train and equip local churches and volunteers to work closely with this population to bring formerly incarcerated persons closer to God. Subsequently, we work with formerly incarcerated persons' family members and connect them with resources to assist their loved ones through the transition period.

Meanwhile, in order for formerly incarcerated individuals to enter back into the community successfully, we believe that certain mechanisms need to be in place and essential resources must be afforded. We believe that our best practices model can be applied broadly to any ministry context focusing on prison ministry. Therefore, below I list and provide details of the programs offered through our Prison Fellowship Ministry, along with our findings.

Connecting Ex-Offenders with Drug Treatment Rehabilitation Programs

At Summerfield we provide formerly incarcerated individuals with drug abuse education. We offer evening programs Monday through Friday taught by seasoned drug abuse instructors contracted through the church. The drug abuse education program consists of a 14-week intensive course funded and operated by the church. Classes are held from 6:00pm-9:00pm. The intention of the class is to provide education regarding substance abuse and its detrimental effects, and seeks to connect individuals with other community resources. This 14-week Therapeutic Substantive-Cognitive Behavioral Rehabilitation course is designed to reverse criminal behavior and to correct poorly developed habits, and provides skill-building opportunities in the areas of institutional and community readjustment, cognitive development, communication skills, interviewing techniques, education support, and detox support for those wanting to withdraw from drug abuse.

We realize that we are a small agency and we are limited in our capacity to offer long-range services, so we work closely with other partner institutions such as the Bridgeport Council of Churches and the Bridgeport Hospital to offer more long-term support. These networks of professionals are able to provide a more comprehensive and long-term treatment program past the 14-week program that Summerfield provides. The Council of Churches and the Bridgeport Hospital offers certified addictions counselors, psychiatrists, psychologist, social workers, professional counselors, medical doctors, chaplains, certified sex offender therapists, sexologists, former substance abuse survivors, etc.. What we have found by offering Summerfield's program over the past two years, and what is evident in our research, is that we have had a 96% success rate in reducing relapse, reducing criminality, and reducing public/private misconduct.

Our model citizens have reported improvements in their overall health, improvements in their relationships, improvements in their cognitive development, and positive improvements in their self-confidence. According to our internal research, we have found job placements for nearly 95% of those we serve, with another 10% returning back to school or seeking a trade. Collectively, these positive outcomes help to reduce the public risk and increase public safety, while also providing an economic benefit to the general public.

Providing a Temporary (30 day) Emergency Shelter
for Those Released from Prison within the Last 30 Days
We understand that housing is critically important to the successful reentry of someone returning home from prison. In the absence of sufficient shelter, a person is more likely to reoffend within the first few weeks of being released according to large bodies of research conducted in this area. Therefore, we aim to provide immediate housing to formerly incarcerated persons

to help with their transition back into the community. Once a person is in our care, then we begin to reach out to other community partners and agencies for more long-term housing support. The unique thing about our church being located in an inner-city, with a plethora of resources targeted at this population, is that affordable housing options are generally scattered throughout the community, thus allowing us to coordinate our efforts towards providing individualized services based upon the specific needs/circumstances of the individual.

For instance, a person released on parole is considered a flight risk to correctional authorities, and therefore has specific housing needs. In such a case, if it is hard for someone who fits this category to find housing, then we work with the Connecticut Department of Corrections in order to provide more intensive supervision during their transition back into the community, while we work with independent landlords within the community to rent a space/room at a more economically affordable rate.

Our team of professionals works closely with various social service agencies throughout the State of Connecticut, and within the City of Bridgeport more specifically, to curtail homelessness. This has allowed us to develop strong and trusting community relationships, which is advantageous to our targeted population. One such example, is partnering with the United States Department of Housing and Urban Development (also known as Section 8) and the Bridgeport Housing Authority, to help expand housing options for formerly incarcerated individuals. These relationships have allowed us to help formerly incarcerated persons and their families to participate in a private market housing option, whereby they receive a federal housing voucher if they fall within a certain economic tax bracket. The voucher serves as supplemental income so families who are already strapped financially do not have to pay out of pocket more than 60% on housing, thus allowing them to pay other household bills and tend to other external obligations (i.e. light bill, water bill, appliances, car insurance, etc.).

Focusing on Measurable Outcomes of Transitional Housing
Through our program tracking and evaluation, we have found that formerly incarcerated individuals are three times more likely to be successful in finding

employment and connecting to educational resources if they have housing than if they do not. We also discovered that they are twice as likely to reconnect with their families when stable housing is in place. We also learned that stable housing decreases the potential for further substance abuse, due to the controls and release stipulations put in place by the federal government/correctional institution for persons recently released from prison.[8] Further, the potential to receive in-house supportive care is greater when a person is in a stable living environment (i.e. certain health care services, in patient procedures, etc.). One of the greatest benefits of providing housing to our model citizens is that it yields crucial long-term benefits. It promotes job stability, strengthens familial connections, aids in character development, promotes public safety, and significantly reduces recidivism.

Creating Healing Communities

Summerfield is dedicated to establishing an atmosphere that seeks to engage formerly incarcerated inmates, their victims, and their families in the restoration process.

Our church community partners with the broader Bridgeport community to provide a safe space where formerly incarcerated individuals feel that they have a community that supports them. Moreover, we are devoted to fostering an environment of radical inclusivity, where people feel valued and respected. We believe that the essential ingredients for cultivating such community must be undergirded by these key principles: compassion, empathy, acceptance, forgiveness, reconciliation, redemption, and mercy. The scriptural text that guides this sacred work is "And be not conformed to this world: but be ye transformed by the renewing of your mind, that ye may prove what is that good, and acceptable, and perfect, will of God" (Rom 12:2).[9]

Seeing People: About Whom Are We Talking?

We believe as articulated in scripture that charity begins at home and then it spreads abroad (1 Tim 5:28). Therefore, with this ideology in mind, we

---

[8] https://csgjusticecenter.org/reentry/issue-areas/housing/.

[9] Representatives of Summerfield UMC are working with the Bridgeport Council of Churches and the Mayor's Initiative for Reentry Affairs to expand our programming in the future to also support victims of crime and their families.

begin by servicing folks in our own community who might be personally affected by incarceration or affected by the incarceration of someone close to them. We seek to serve both the individual and the families who have to interface or be confronted by the realities of the criminal justice system. We serve as a bridge builder between formerly incarcerated individuals and their families. For example, we seek to connect mothers and fathers to their children, spouses to their partners, and children to their extended family members, while providing spiritual support to all who need it. Toward that end, we believe that a part of creating a healing community is being present with people on their journey. At Summerfield we do not allow any person to "walk alone."

The church community at Summerfield is extremely compassionate and welcomes everyone with open arms, an open heart, and an open mind. We are a community that does not make people feel bad about their prior life choices and decisions. In fact, we embrace the total person: the good, the bad, and the ugly, because we know what shame, stigma, and fear does to the human spirit.

In an effort to promote human flourishing, we work with individuals to help them take responsibility for their lives and encourage them to take action in paying their debt back to society, their victims, and their families by leading productive lives and by showing remorse through the act of giving back to the community and not returning to a life of crime. Lastly, we believe that our church community has a biblical mandate of leading the charge on prison ministry in Bridgeport. Therefore, we have turned our ministry inside out; which basically means that our parishioners understand that church is not relegated to the four walls of the church; we must be God's hands and feet to the world by engaging with those on the margins and those who are considered "the least of these" by our society.

There are seven core community framework pieces that we think are vital in creating healthy and effective healing communities: I will list these seven areas first and then provide a brief description of each.

- **Education:** Congregations must work to educate people on crime and its effects on the community, one's personal life, one's health, and one's future potential. Congregations must educate people on the general laws/ordinances governing each state, municipality, local jurisdiction, while simultaneously educating people on the criminal justice concerns in one's local community/municipal context.

- **Leadership:** Congregations must identify leaders in helping point people to broader community resources, and at the same time be responsible for implementing effective programs germane to the church's outreach ministries in this area.

- **Community Partners/Stakeholders:** Congregations must work together with other churches, civic organizations, for-profit and not-for-profit entities in helping to give birth to an alternative community, where justice, love, mercy and peace abound. The idea is for these various entities to come together to create a community where people feel safe, vulnerable to share their experiences, and to share a meal with one another. These community partners would form a prayer circle or engage in other shared learning opportunities as a way to reinforce the value of personal and collective accountability.

- **Outreach and Radical Inclusion:** Congregations must get outside of the church and be willing to get their hands dirty. Instead of people finding the church, churches must go find the people and to compel them to come in. Therefore, congregations and church leaders must preach and teach grace and mercy everywhere they go and must not forget the importance of spreading the message of love as personified by Jesus Christ. Congregations must take the initiative of creating a structure and culture of healing by empowering people through the art of storytelling.

- **Congregational Empowerment:** Congregations should view the issue of incarceration as a public safety and public health concern. It does not matter whether or not this is an agenda item for a particular congregation, nor does it matter where your church is situated – be it in the ghetto, inner-city, or the suburbs – congregations and leaders must view the issue of incarceration as a humanitarian crisis and must work to create more healthy communities. The mandate therefore is for well-to-do congregations devoid of a social justice agenda and who may be focusing on other issues (such as saving the environment or protecting wildlife), to unclench their fist and to extend their hands outwardly toward ministries that are engaged in this work. Conversely, ministries that are engaged in prison ministry must be willing to educate others on how the issue of incarceration impacts one's community.

- **Development of Service Minded Volunteers:** Congregations must solicit the participation of volunteers to help spread the message of inclusion to those who feel that the church is beyond their reach. Volunteers must spread a consistent message with respect to their church's individualized/personalized healing community structure. Volunteers must share the responsibility of providing support to individuals and their families looking to be transformed and reintegrated back into the community.

- **Empower and Equip Formerly Incarcerated Individuals to Have Agency:** Congregations must empower and equip formerly incarcerated persons within and outside of their congregation to take control of their own lives by sharing their life's journey through participation with other formerly incarcerated individuals through a long-term mentoring process. This process can take place over the course of a few weeks or be broken down through a series of weekend retreats. At Summerfield this work takes place over the course of 4 weekends broken down quarterly. The program begins in our social hall and ends with a community service project in conjunction with the Bridgeport Police Department through our Youth Violence Prevention Initiative partnership. Typically, the pastor and a few SPRC (Staff Parish Relations Committee) members are a part of this process.

We offer mentoring to at-risk youth and formerly incarcerated youth who have gone through the Connecticut Juvenile Justice System.

Connecting Formerly Incarcerated Individuals with Jobs/Employers in the Community

Summerfield provides three orientation trainings for those seeking employment in the Bridgeport community. We also provide a total of 10 weeks over the course of the summer for job readiness training through our Youth with a Purpose Program (YWAP). We refer applicants with no work history into transitional jobs through the Bridgeport Employment Temp Service. Our team of professionals also assists with resume building and works closely with the internet site CareerBuilder, where formerly incarcerated individuals can upload their resumes and get interviews. Once every two months we host a one-stop-shop workshop where we bring employers from around the City of Bridgeport and greater Fairfield County to discuss employment opportunities. We also engage in mock skype interviews with potential employers to help returning citizens acclimate to using virtual technologies.

Summerfield also partners with outside agencies that provide more hard skill training for those looking for a trade. This training has the potential to lead to careers in construction, cosmetology, packaging, and certain environmental engineering jobs. Summerfield also works collaboratively with the Bridgeport Board of Education and Housatonic Community College to help individuals earn their high school diploma and GED, so that they are more marketable and competitive in the job market. Once participants complete our job training program, they are automatically matched with employers, and we provide a small stipend to participants after the completion of 90 days on a job.

In addition to providing formerly incarcerated individuals with job and skills training, we also provide crises intervention counseling for those suffering from anxiety disorder, spiritual and mental depression, adjustment issues, and any other issues affecting one's emotional, physical, or psychological state of being. Our trained professionals pay special attention to behavior. By doing so, we are able to identify areas of vulnerability and areas in one's life that makes one more susceptible to engaging in self-destructing actions.

Connect Formerly Incarcerated Individuals with Educational Opportunities and Walk Them Through the Difficult College Admissions Process

At Summerfield we believe that education is the bridge to the future and the cornerstone of our democracy. Research shows that education has the potential to lift one and one's family out of poverty.[10] With this in mind, we work tirelessly to close the achievement/educational gap. We believe that when people are educated and have something to look forward to, they are less likely to engage in street-level crime and are less of a risk to public safety.

In 2015, we established a formal partnership with Housatonic Community College in helping formerly incarcerated individuals prepare for the rigorous college admissions process. As a result of this partnership, Housatonic's admissions staff, along with current students at Housatonic, assist interested individuals in preparing a strong admissions application. In 2016, Summerfield helped to place 16 formerly incarcerated individuals into colleges and universities around the State of Connecticut and received a proclamation from the Bridgeport Mayor's Office for our efforts.

The Impact of Summerfield's Program

As a college admissions administrator myself, I have had the pleasure of helping 25 formerly incarcerated individuals applying to college gain admittance over the span of only two years. This means more than 90% of those I have helped prepare their college application were accepted to college and have matriculated successfully into their second year at the community college level. While this is certainly a milestone, we must continue to shatter the glass ceiling for those whose backs are against the wall and have been otherwise shut out of society. It is here that I think it is important to share the testimonials and success stories from those who have gone through Summerfield's Prison Fellowship Program. You will find an abbreviated version of their stories below. The stories are true and authentic ex-

---

[10] The University of Chicago Campaign Inquiry and Impact," https://campaign.uchicago.edu/.

pressions written directly by those served by Summerfield's Prison Fellowship Program.

Abandoned by Parents at Age Seven: Mike, July 2017

My name is Mike, affectionately known as Micky. My parents abandoned me when I was only seven years of age. I remember my mother saying she never wanted to be pregnant with me because I reminded her of my father who was a chronic alcoholic. My father also gambled and mistreated my mother and my two older sisters. Because I looked a lot like my father, my mother saw me as the bastard child and put me into foster care.

From the age of seven until about fifteen, I lived from house to house. Some of the homes I was placed in I was physically assaulted, verbally abused, and was forced to work or sell my body in order to help pay utilities. I was left to the streets to take care of me. I got hooked up with the wrong crowd and quickly turned to the life of the streets.

I literally lived by the streets and ultimately wanted to die by the streets. In fact, the people on the street treated me better than people in my own family, or better yet the people the government put in charge to take care of me. At the age of thirteen I encountered the criminal justice system for stealing and armed robbery. I was sentenced to three years in "juvey" followed by three years of probation. At the age of 22, I was sentenced to prison for selling drugs to an undercover police officer. I spent eight years in jail for that and now at age 30 I am trying to get my life back on track.

After meeting Pastor Gaston from Summerfield while I was finishing out my sentence, I decided that once I get out of prison I would visit his church and see if he could help me. A month after I was released, I started going to Summerfield and learning more about God, and since that time, my life has been on the up and up. Pastor Gaston's witness has helped to convert me into being a better man. He helped me to realize that to a certain extent I must take responsibility for my past indiscretions and to not blame myself for the terrible childhood I inherited. This was a turning point for me. For the first time, I felt a glimmer of hope.

This past year, Pastor Gaston helped me to enroll in school and I am now finishing up my first semester of college. Pastor Gaston helped to reconnect me with my high school sweetheart and now we are on the road towards marriage. Two weeks ago, on June 25, Maria and I got engaged. I am now assisting Pastor Gaston at Summerfield in the area of outreach ministry, and working to establish a group home for foster kids. I would like to thank Pastor Gaston and others who have poured into my life in deeply profound ways. I truly feel redeemed from a life of crime, and I am ready to make a positive difference in the world.

I Am Ashamed of What I Did: Timothy, July 2017

My name is Timothy and I am 33 years old. I was recently released from Connecticut State Prison after serving five years in prison for molestation. I was married to a nice young lady whom I had known for ten years leading up to my arrest. We had two beautiful children together and one step daughter.

My wife, Tiffany, and I were going through some issues in our marriage early on and promised to work through them. However, we never really found the time to do so. Tiffany worked crazy hours for a retail store and most of my hours were spent working in a local church in New Britain, Connecticut as a choir director/musician. For some reason, I connected more with the youth at the church than with my own wife, especially since many of them were close in age to me.

And to be honest, I was 33 years old, but still very immature. The average student in the choir was closer to seventeen. One day the pastor was preaching about how it is perfectly fine to express vulnerability and to open up to others about things that are bothering us. Consequently, I made the silly mistake of confiding in one of the female youth from the choir because she was the only person that seemed to understand me. Regrettably, our relationship grew closer to the point that boundaries were crossed.

I felt so embarrassed by this single incident that I felt obligated to share it with the senior pastor of the church, and of course, he was obligated to report it to the authorities. As I imagined, the entire situation blew up and I was later arrested and prosecuted. My then wife Tiffany wasted no time filing for a divorce, and I was left to support myself. The entire church community abandoned me. The pastor told me that I had fallen from grace and that God would not forgive me for what I had done. Every day while I was behind bars, I could not find it in me to forgive myself.

However, closer to the time of my release, I heard about Pastor Gaston and his advocacy around prison ministry from one of the chaplains of the prison. I asked Chaplain Steel if he could make the connection and that I would love to meet and talk with him, especially around forgiveness. Three weeks later Pastor Gaston visited me and gave me several key scriptures to read to begin the process of healing. He also expressed to me his passion to serve God's people. He even went as far as to share his own incarceration experience with me, which was one of the most incredible and powerful stories I had ever witnessed in my life. He promised to walk with me and to support me post my release from prison, and invited me to learn more about his Prison Fellowship Program.

When I was released in March of 2017, I found Pastor Gaston's contact information and reached out to him. He helped to find housing for me in Bridgeport through the Bridgeport Council of Churches, and assisted me in finding a job. Four months later, I am working a part-time job and seeking educational opportunities.

Although I am ashamed of my past, Pastor Gaston reminds me that my future is brighter than my past, and so with this motivation and support, I now believe that I am not beyond God's saving grace and redemptive power.

Turning My Life Around: Rebecca, July 2017

My name is Rebecca. I am a former addict. At the age of twelve I begin experimenting with drugs and alcohol. By the age of sixteen I had my sixth child all from different fathers. All of my kids were taken from me by DCF. This caused me to develop anxiety disorder and manic depression, which led to me committing crimes and using more drugs. I found that by using drugs lessened my anxiety, but at the same time, it contributed to me making bad choices. At the age of 18, I was sentenced to four years in prison for the selling cannabis to an undercover cop. At that point, I was considered unfit to have any interactions with my kids in the DCF system. After serving my sentence, I was released from prison and was briefly living with my mother from Ansonia, Connecticut until she no longer wanted me to live there. In March

2017, I moved to Bridgeport after learning about Section 8 opportunities for formerly incarcerated persons.

At that time, I heard about Rev. Gaston's program at Summerfield and requested to join the network. Rev. Gaston allowed me to join his program and after six weeks of attending trainings and workshops around jobs, I landed a position working for a nonprofit organization in Bridgeport, and now I am looking to start a new family. Summerfield's Prison Fellowship Program saved my life. In the absence of this support, I could easily see myself returning to a life of crime. Summerfield's staff is very resourceful and is respected throughout the City of Bridgeport. Rev. Gaston personally connected me with the president from Housatonic Community College and I am hoping to enroll in school this upcoming spring semester. I have also joined Rev. Gaston's ministry as a result of his commitment to my transition back into the community.

Crime, I've Done It All: Roderick, July 2017

Roderick here. I heard about Summerfield's Prison Fellowship Program six months before being released from Connecticut State Prison. Rev. Gaston and a few clergy from Bridgeport came to speak with us about options on the outside once we were released. Rev. Gaston gave me his business card and information about his church, so when I got out, I hit him up and scheduled an appointment to meet with him. During our appointment, he told me that he saw the light of God in me and advised me to stay out of trouble.

My entire life I have been in and out of jail. The first time I went to jail was for domestic violence, the second time I went to jail I went for selling drugs, and the last time I went to jail it was for armed robbery. If you add up all the time I spent it jail, it was like a total of fifteen years and I am barely even thirty years old. Anyways to make a long story short, Rev. Gaston helped me out a lot. He helped to find me a job. He helped me write my resume. He helped me believe in myself again, and he helped to teach me more about God. Now I am a part of his ministry because I see the heart of God in him, and the people of Summerfield—they are committed to my success as a young black man.

Me and Rev. Gaston are now looking for ways for me to get back in school. I think that if I get back in school then I would be able to get a better job in order to take care of myself. I do not want to return to the streets, but the way that society is set up, it kind of makes it hard not to. I hope to one day have a family and to teach my kids the right way because growing up I did not have a role model, or anyone that looked out for you, you feel me? So now that I am a man—I appreciate all the help I am receiving from Summerfield Prison Fellowship Program.

From Feeling Like A Nobody to Feeling Like A Somebody: Jerry, July 2017
My name is Jerry. I was released from prison 6 months ago after serving 25 years. Upon my release the only thing I was given was a tee shirt, a pair of ripped jeans, a baseball cap, and a thirty-dollar voucher. It was an entire new world out there. I have had never used the internet in all of my life. In fact, I am still having difficulties using the internet and using a cell phone. Nobody ever told me that my life would change this much. I would rather be back in prison because it is easier. I have no family. I have no kids. I have no job. I am just living from place to place.

A few weeks ago, I learned about Summerfield United Methodist Church's Prison Fellowship Program. I became a part of the program after meeting with Rev. Gaston and discussing my options. He indicated that he would help me to enroll in school and personally took me to Housatonic Community College, and assisted me with filling out my application and I was admitted on the spot. I have now joined Rev. Gaston's ministry and is working with young people in his Youth with a Purpose Program, designed to keep young people on the straight and narrow path. In the absence of Summerfield's Prison Fellowship Program, I would probably be back in the system.

Finding Hope in God: Tiffany. July 2017
In year 2000, I was arrested for running a major drug operation from out of my church. I served seventeen years in federal prison. While in prison I lost contact with my family who is originally from Bridgeport. I was recently released from federal prison in June and since that time have been trying to get on my feet. I learned about Summerfield's Prison Fellowship Program

and immediately caught the City bus to find more information about the program. The friendly staff at Summerfield explained the program to me in detail, and told me that had three openings left. I applied and immediately they placed me in temporary housing.

A few weeks later they helped me apply to Section 8 housing, and found me a placement. I am now in the process of applying to jobs across Fairfield County. SUMC's Prison Fellowship program assisted me in writing my resume, cover letter, and are willing to provide me with a reference letter. I went from not getting any calls back from employers to being invited to interviews. Although I don't have a job as of yet, I am optimistic that I will find something soon. Summerfield's Prison Fellowship Program provides me with three meals a day and a bus voucher to get around the City.

They also assist me with other personal things I need such as deodorant, hygiene products, and a weekly stipend. I attend Sunday worship with Summerfield each Sunday and my spiritual life is growing. I now hope to attend seminary so that I can help other people find God. My life is nothing short of a miracle. I should not be on this earth, but I must be placed here for a reason, and I would like to help other young women avoid the prison system. With the help of Rev. Gaston and others, I hope to start a nonprofit that will focus on the holistic health of women.

My Life Has Not Been a Crystal Stair: Thomas, August 2017

My name is Thomas, and I would like to tell you about my life journey. For over twenty years I lived with fear, rejection, denial, addiction, and poor choices. As a child I was extremely selfish. I made some really silly mistakes. I use to steal from my grandmother which eventually led to me stealing from a grocery store. My grandmother provided everything for me and my siblings, but it was easier for me to rebel. I truly lived a double life. The double life I lived was good vs. evil. I knew right from wrong, but I simply wanted to choose the evil side of me. I grew up in church but I was tired of seeing people around me suffering and God never coming to their rescue.

To be honest, contrary to my upbringing in the church, I questioned God and doubted the existence of God. I spent many years in and out of jail and treatment centers. I honestly did not care to confront reality. It wasn't until

I was sentenced to twenty-four years in prison that I found my faith again. In fact, it was all I had if I was going to survive my long prison sentence. It was behind bars that I reconnected with God. However, there were times when I attempted suicide. In my cell, I attempted to choke myself to death. I wanted out. Then again, God stepped in and didn't allow me to take myself out. It was at this point that I gave myself to a higher power. I have been blessed ever since.

Running into Pastor Gaston after my release from prison was symbolic of God ordering my steps. Summerfield's Prison Fellowship Program helped me to believe in myself again. I finally got a job for the first time in my life! Summerfield's job training program is unprecedented. It has gotten my life back on track, and now I feel that a new ministry has been birthed inside of me. For the rest of my adult life, I plan to work for the church and to help as many people as I can avoid going to prison. Christ paid the price for all of our freedom, and there is more to life than residing behind bars. I have joined Rev. Gaston's ministry and I know that my life is only going to go up from here.

Gaining My Strength Back: Regina, August 2017

A few months ago, while in Connecticut State Prison, I heard about Rev. Herron Gaston from the prison chaplain of the jail. I spoke with him about returning to Bridgeport after serving my sentence, and he told me about Summerfield United Methodist Churches Prison Fellowship Program. I decided to contact Rev. Gaston two weeks after returning to the community. He and his staff were really helpful in helping me to create a long-term plan for my future. I enrolled in his job training program and three months later I was working at his church in the food pantry as a pantry assistant. Rev. Gaston paid me bi-weekly and assisted me in finding affordable housing in the community. Today, I still work for the church and am slowly getting back on my feet. Summerfield's Prison Fellowship Project is one of a kind. There are other programs similar to this one in Bridgeport but I have not found them to be particularly useful. I am interested in getting a trade, and Rev. Gaston has promised to help me enroll in vocational school within the next year. So with this in mind, my focus has been on becoming a successful entrepreneur and to eventually get married and have a family. I am happy to be a part of Summerfield's ministry and I know that with the support of the people at the church that I am in good hands. I have reestablished a relationship with God and with God I know that all things are possible.

Summary

Summerfield United Methodist Church has a long history – from its very beginnings – of commitment to social justice in word and deed. Recognizing that formerly incarcerated persons can regain a sense of self and belonging, that they can trust they are contributing members of the community, has been the hallmark of Summerfield's prison ministry. By focusing on the human person in all his/her needs (physical, mental, emotional, spiritual), we have been able to help facilitate healing and reintegration. The Summerfield Prison Reentry program inspired this project and the hope that the UMC and the greater Christian community can follow our lead in bringing true restoration and reconciliation to those who have been imprisoned and their families.

CHAPTER FIVE

Methodological Strategy and Research Summaries

Introduction

The purpose of this project was to explore and establish a blueprint for the United Methodist Church based on the current Mission Plan for Restorative Justice Ministries (MPRJM) that could be used internally or externally within the United Methodist Church and beyond to deal with the flux of ex-prisoners from the criminal justice system returning back to the community. The blueprint can be used by other United Methodist Churches and other denominations to begin to deal with the issues associated with prison reentry and restorative justice. In particular, the United Methodist Church is poised to lead in this area due to their creed, structural and connectional emphasis on mission work, outreach, and methodical steadfastness to deliver and foster justice and the restorative process among former prisoners. Thus, the initial question as to who will be there to receive them in a restorative fashion rested on the history and focus of the United Methodist Church's commitment to support for prisoners and ex-prisoners.

The project utilized a three-step qualitative approach – focus groups, individual interviews, and interview transcription – to ascertain information from United Methodist parishioners at the Summerfield United Methodist Church in Bridgeport, Connecticut and from leaders in the Connecticut/New York District to collect their views to the four Guiding Questions and how those questions and responses fit within the current United Methodist Church and its Mission Plan for Restorative Justice Ministries (MPRJM), at which level action could be realized.

A review of the current United Methodist Church's Mission Plan for Restorative Justice Ministries (MPRJM) was used to set the tone and basis for the blueprint and to call attention and action to this plan in light of the burgeoning increases in the prison population, the rise and complexity of the prison industrial complex, and the support and restoration of ex-prisoners returning back to the community. Ideas and thoughts of parishioners were gathered during a separate interview session using the four guiding questions as the focal ideas to be explored.

The research approach sought to gather input based on the topic of prison ministry/reentry and the perceived role of the church in general and the United Methodist Church in specific. Therefore, Step 1 (Focus Group Session) allowed for parishioners to be introduced to the project and to understand what their interest or views were in relationship to prison ministry, prisoners returning back to the community, and the role of the United Methodist Church. Step 2 (Individual Interview) consisted of one-on-one conversations of some of those who were in attendance and agreed to be interviewed and to elaborate and respond personally to the four guiding project questions discussed in Chapter 1 and again at the beginning of Chapter 4.

Challenges and Opportunities of Qualitative Research

There are certain limitations associated with any research design or approach and this study was no exception to those dilemmas. There are even more limitations when using focus groups and personal interviews in a church setting, and then transcribing the responses. Qualitative research can be described generally as investigative methodologies and techniques that offer naturalistic, phonological[11], ethnographic, or observer focused information. This research approach is used across many disciplines with varying approaches and designs in gathering data to respond to a group of questions.

---

[11] According to dictionary.com: "the study of the distribution and patterning of speech sounds in a language and of the tacit rules governing pronunciation."

A variety of techniques such as case studies, interviews, personal observations and focus groups are among those used in a variety of contexts including mixed methodologies that include some degree of both qualitative and quantitative strategies. Among the limitations and disadvantages of qualitative research is that this type of research is heavily dependent on the skills of the researcher and may be easily influenced by personal biases. Another limitation or disadvantage of qualitative research designs is that rigidity is more difficult to assess, demonstrate, and maintain. This type of design is also time consuming and interpretation can be quite difficult. Often times this type of research is not readily accepted in the larger scientific community and the presence of the researcher in the process can cause a certain degree of subjectivity; therefore, objectivity can be decreased or compromised. Issues of confidentiality and difficulty in displaying the findings can also be problematic for the researcher.

Despite these many limitations, there are several advantages and strengths to using this type of approach. One major advantage is that participants can be evaluated indepth and one can ascertain many details unavailable in a quantitative approach. Another advantage or strength is that direction and framework can be altered and changed quickly as new information emerges. One of the greatest advantages given this topic is that qualitative research focuses on the lived experiences of individuals within their context or living environments and can have rich and compelling outcomes. Further, since data is usually collected from only a few people, cases, or situations, it cannot be generalized to the larger population. Yet, the findings can be transferred to other like settings. Finally, this method helps the researcher get a smaller portion of the bigger picture given their focus and problem under investigation.

I employed the focus group strategy as the first step in the process to bring awareness to the conversation about prison reentry ministry, and to address the core question poised in introduction: "Who will be there to receive them in a restorative fashion?" The focus group strategy was followed by steps 2 and 3, individual recorded interviews and final transcription of responses verbatim.

Core Question and Guiding Questions

This project provided greater insight into the views and perceptions of church parishioners and leaders within the United Methodist Church about the role of the United Methodist Church in prison reentry ministries and support while clarifying who is obligated to support ex-prisoners upon their exit from the criminal justice system back in to the community. The core question poised in Chapter 1, "Who will be there to receive them in a restorative fashion?" was presented rhetorically to the Christian community to explore the general thoughts about the epic problem of mass incarceration, the prison industrial complex, and the masses expected to exit the prions system and return back to their respective communities. It is the role of Christians and the faith community to be in a position, as well as understand their mandate, to receive these individuals and provide them with spiritual support and also clothing, shelter, and food. Parishioners shared that it is the duty and responsibility of the Church, but particularly the United Methodist Church, to play a greater role in this process.

Focus Group and Interview Sample Participants

The focus group session took place in May 2017 in the Hall of the Summerfield United Methodist Church by invitation at the end of church service. A group of 25 parishioners of varying socioeconomic backgrounds and gender were present. I facilitated the session, and the main topics of conversation centered on our current prison fellowship ministry and whether or not members believed that we were making a difference in our own community. There were no structured questions for this session as it was used primarily to begin dialogue about prison reentry ministries and the role of the United Methodist Church. This focus group lasted for approximately 45 minutes and members were asked if they wished to participate in an interview to respond the four guiding questions. The interview stage consisted of nine (9) parishioners agreeing to be interviewed between May – June, 2017. Seven of the nine answered all of the questions and two of the participants only answered question #1. For the benefit of consistency and completeness, I have only included the seven parishioners who responded to all of the four questions. The full results can be found in the appendix section of this document.

Step 1: The Focus Group

The focus group methodology is a form of qualitative research that has a long history in the worlds of marketing, retail, urban planning, and in the social sciences which date back to the early 1940s (Leung & Savithiri, 2009). A focus group essentially involves bringing people together and assessing their attitudes or views about a certain product, issue, or a set of questions. Focus group participants usually are asked a series of questions or in some cases, only one question. It is expected that questions be short, natural, and open-ended (Leung & Savithiri, 2009). Focus groups have become very popular as an effective needs assessment tool in fields like healthcare, education, and business (Leung & Savithiri, 2009; Mansel, Bennett, Northway, Mead, & Moseley, 2004).

Step 2 & 3: Interview and Transcription of Results

Participants were asked the four Guiding Questions:

1 How can the United Methodist Church play a greater role in assisting with prison reentry and restorative justice?
2 How can the leadership and connectional mission of the United Methodist Church be used to create a blueprint for restorative justice programs through its connectional system?
3 What is the role of the leaders of the United Methodist Church in training, preparing, and empowering its laity for restorative justice and reentry activities within its current structure?
4 What should churches be trained to do in order to deal with prison reentry and restorative justice programs?

The names of the parishioners who participated in individual interviews have been protected using term Parishioner 1-7. Their responses to the "Guiding Questions for the Call to Action" are recorded verbatim below.

Individual Responses to the Guiding Questions

A total of nine parishioners were interviewed, however only seven answered all of the interview questions. A summary of their responses are provided below for each question.

Question 1: How can the United Methodist Church play a greater role in assisting with prison reentry and restorative justice? It seemed clear that the overarching response to this question centered around the fact the United Methodist Church must play an even greater role and that a good deal of that role should be based on relationship development with other congregations in the area outside of the United Methodist Church's connectional system. For example, Parishioner 1 responded in the following manner and offered her idea of what needed to be done:

> The United Methodist Church can play an even greater role with prison reentry by focusing more squarely on developing closer relationships with other local congregations (outside of the UMC connectional system) in addressing the needs of the formerly incarcerated population. This way, we will be able to address multiple facets of prison ministry with within the context of a vast church community. In other words, we need to better connect and pool our resources with other organizations/agencies/partners within local neighborhoods and work alongside the ongoing work in the community to which our local churches sit, as a way to identify assets in the community to successfully reintegrated formerly incarcerated inmates.

Parishioner 2 suggested a uniform program for reentry since there is no standard for what all churches should do. This would be quite helpful in evaluating and determining success of such programs within the United Methodist Church structure.

Parishioner 2 stated:

> The UMC church should create a uniform reentry program that focuses keenly on programs that addresses the needs of

prison inmates upon them being released. I think each parish should be devoted to creating a space/ or a center that gives them a place to live, grow, and develop in their faith while providing them with opportunities to find a job, transportation to and from work, along with a secure place to live and assisting them with the job search process. We need to help people to feel self-reliant and productive citizens of society who has something to offer their respective community, their families, and themselves.

In the eyes of this parishioner, the United Methodist Church should take more seriously its Mission Plan and create uniformity, synergy, and organized centers of support to help ex-prisoners and their families with jobs and work with them on being productive self-reliant citizens. Like Parishioner 3, this person believes that collaboration would be essential to a cohesive and comprehensive program for prison reentry. However, Parishioner 3 felt the leadership needed to be involved, trained, and educated at the local level to take on this task. Parishioner 3 noted the following:

The UMC church must learn to work more collaboratively with other institutions, organizations, and ministries that is already doing this work and are producing tangible results. I think whenever we work on something as large as the prison issue, we need all hands-on deck. Besides, each faith community looks differently and the needs are all different. There is no one size fit all. The UMC church could afford to be more proactive than reactive when it comes to reentry initiatives. We need to continuously send our leadership to training, and the leadership needs to provide that training or educational experience back into the local church. The leadership of the church should not just arm local clergy with handling this complex aspect of ministry, but they, themselves, (speaking of the leaders) should get at eye-level with this population as well by engaging more on the ground instead of brainstorming in the ivory tower or some lofty conference room space in a distant hotel.

Parishioner 4 felt that there must be strong connections within the community, especially the business community which may need to work to hire these persons. Particularly, the church should reconcile these ex-prisoners in the grace of God and restore them. Parishioner 4 stated:

> At the forefront of any reentry programs must be grounded in meaningful connections with the business community, such that the end of reentry programs are employability. Such that the end is reconciliation the Church must see this as a central part of its ministry, bringing people into reconciliation with one another and by that greater reconciliation with God. Practically this looks like a leveraging Church investments on a national level toward enticing business owners to hire formerly incarcerated persons and establishing our congregations as Accessible and Affirming spaces for them.

Like Parishioner 4 who believes in the role of the business community and the church reconciling in the name of God, Parishioner 5 felt that to create more synergy and involvement, there should be a "think tank" created to bring the ideas under one central response to prison reentry and to work with local, state, and national leaders through legislation and other policy changes to ensure their success upon reentry back into the community. Parishioner 5 stated "The United Methodist Church should create a public policy "think tank" that works very closely with state, local, and national leaders in implementing smart, common sense legislation to help create diversion programs that will put people back to work and reorient them into the life of their respective communities."

Parishioners 5 and 6 shared common themes in terms of working outside of the church, realizing that the church cannot take on this task alone. Again, they both focused on jobs, employment readiness, collaboration, and partnership building without recreating the wheel. Parishioner 6 stated the following:

> The United Methodist Church should work closely to identify corporations and businesses who will hire ex-prisoners upon their release within the community. The UMC church must also work with local community colleges in the community to offer ex-prisoners a vocation or a certificate program that will allow them to compete in the job market. They must also get outside of the local church and to pair with other organizations who is working towards a similar goal. It makes no sense to reinvent the wheel.

Parishioner 7 focused more on the initial transitional needs of the prisoner upon reentry and that the church should help them with this transition and teach them certain skills, create relationships, and help them to begin to think differently in an effort to reduce recidivism. Thus, Parishioner 7 said, "The United Methodist Church should help them with transitioning. They need to teach people how to use the cell phone, the internet, and other technological advancements. Churches must work to reduce recidivism. We need to value people and create strong relationships. We must help people to think differently and must put people to work."

Overall, the parishioners' responses to *Guiding Question 1* renewed our understanding and the role of the United Methodist Church in prison reentry programs and efforts. Each believed it was indeed the role of the church to help in a variety of ways such as: building partnerships with all sectors of the community and other congregations (UMC and non-UMC), providing support both practical and spiritual, teaching new skills for survival, and supporting self-reliance in each of these efforts. All parishioners responded to this question except parishioner 7. Therefore, it will not be included.

Question 2: How can the leadership and connectional mission of the United Methodist Church be used to create a blueprint for restorative justice programs through its connectional system? Regarding question 2, which focused specifically on the leadership and the connectional mission of the church to help create a blueprint for restorative justice programs, parishioners felt very strongly about what the leadership's role should be in this effort to establish a clear blueprint for action going forward.

Parishioner 1 shared the following:

> The UMC church boasts about having a large number of prison chaplains, wardens, and other prison reformers. These criminal justice practitioners also hold key leadership positions within their respective local congregations. One way in which the leadership of the UMC church can create a model blueprint for restorative justice program is by utilizing our vast amount of human resources. It would be great to propose as an idea at General Conference—to create a "prison reentry think-tank," comprised of correctional professionals, law enforcement, wardens, parole officers, probation officers, and other criminal justice players to collaborate under one roof and to brainstorm about ways in which to create an alternate reality for prisoners. At present, the UMC church is in a good position to lead the " faith based reentry" charge because of its ecclesial commitment to protecting and standing against all forms of injustice as we endeavor to create holistic healing communities with an aim to set the captives free and to restore them spiritually back to wholeness.

Here, Parishioner 1 almost makes a mockery of the well-structured system of the United Methodist Church and its ability to do so many things, saying the Church should really think about its structure and leadership allocation given this issue, and suggested the General Conference be used to convene a "think-tank." Parishioner 2 focused on these ideas but pushed the more ecclesiastical perspective and the duty of God's people to do this work. Parishioner 2 also noted the structure already in place and the large voluntary force to do this job and take on this task as it has taken on so many other causes. Parishioner 2 shared the following:

The United Methodist Church is devoted and committed from an ecclesial perspective and its foundational beliefs that prisoners are an integral part of God's beloved community. Therefore, this being the general ethos of the institutional church's mission, speaks to the character and personality of the UMC church on a whole. The UMC already has a target population (men, women, children, juveniles, and families). We already have skilled and talented men and women within our ranks who have done this type of work over the span of their careers. We have eager volunteers to help assist in this area of the churches adopted mission.

Like Parishioner 1 and Parishioner 2, Parishioner 3 noted the Church's vast amount of resources and structure, and its need to work at all levels and even with the White House Faith Based Office to be more inclusive and be the leader in this conversation. Parishioner 3 had the following response:

The UMC church has tons of resources within the connectional system. Local clergy should be required to attend at least one/two trainings in this area a year, regardless of the individual mission of their local parish. In 2012, there were more UMC clergy/laity working in the White House Faith Based Office than folks represented from other denominations. Therefore, the UMC church is in a unique position to lead the conversation on how to engage this very complex issue the best.

Parishioner 4 expanded the role of the leadership to focus on funding, the structure, and many ideas that the Church has to rethink about prison reentry ministries to coordinate resources better to achieve such goals. Parishioner 4 noted the following in their response:

On a funding level the connectional structure of the Church can lend itself toward innovative funding ideas, particularly as we explore where to focus our missional spending. More-over, it has the possibility of pushing us toward rethinking how congregations interact intra-communally toward the planning of events and coordinating of resources to assist in fostering restorative justice locally. It may also provide an opportunity for Churches without pastors or with dwin-dling memberships to see new ministry opportunities in connection with their sister congregations toward a realiza-tion of Christ's beloved community.

According to Parishioner 5, resource allocation should be focused outside of the U.S. and focus ministries on churches who are facing crisis and work more with correctional facilities. They shared the following

> The UMC church should spend more resources in this area opposed to focusing on issues outside of the US context. This means that we need to redirect our priorities to ad-dress this crucial aspect of ministry that many in our urban churches are facing. This is also an issue for those living in our suburban communities, as for many of our con-stituents either work for a correctional facility, or have one in our backyard. In other words, all of us are complicit and culpable either directly or indirectly in this issue of mass incarceration.

Parishioner 6 felt that leadership should look at reorganizing the small-large church set-up and find more cost effective and creative ways to solve issues. Thus, promoting effective ministries regardless of the mission was a clear thought of Parishioner 6. The following statement is Parishioner 6's response to guiding question 2: "Smaller churches with large endowments should think about merging with other churches that are doing the practical work of ministry. We must find creative ways to pool our resources together to en-sure that it is going to good use—instead of just holding the doors of a church open and the ministry is ineffective."

Question 3: What is the role of the leaders of the United Methodist Church in training, preparing, and empowering its laity for restorative justice and reentry activities within its current structure? Responses to *Guiding Question 3* were diverse but primarily focused on the perceptions of the role of the leaders of the United Methodist Church in the training, preparation, and empowerment of the laity in regards to restorative justice and reentry activities within the current system. The responses are presented below.

Parishioner 1 felt the United Methodist Church had an ethical and moral obligation to challenge the system and the leaders must engage in this through their own doctrine of God and their mandate as Christian leaders. Parishioner 1 stated the following:

> Leaders within the UMC church has a moral and ethical obligation to speaking truth to power and to challenge systems of dominance with bold proclivity. Rooted in a prophetic tradition of isolating and challenging what is understood to be deeply flawed and morally defective is paramount to understanding the character of the UMC church. The role of leaders in the UMC church are to be "moral agitators" committed to justice. Moreover, the role of the church is to create compassion ministries that equip the laity and other faith leaders within the church to work within and outside of the church and to truly be God's hands and feet to the world. Local clergy should be in the business of equipping leaders with knowledge of the Bible around our shared/individual obligation as moral agents to pursue and to seek God's justice. It is incumbent upon us to foster and forge healing communities, thus providing an intimate setting necessary for spiritual growth. Hence, the ethos of the UMC church believe that God is in such close solidarity and identification with the wounded, sick, poor, and imprisoned that what is done to them is done to God (Matt. 25:31-46). At the heart of God's nature is reconciliation. God was in Christ recon-

ciling the world unto Godself and calling the church as an agent of reconciliation (II Cor. 5:16-21).

"I shall endeavor to show, "said John Wesley, "that Christianity is essentially as social religion, and that to turn it into a solitary one is to destroy it." With characteristic directness he then spelled out for his followers the specific methods they could employ to avoid this dangerous pitfall of solitariness. In the General Rules of 1743, he urged Methodist to practice words of mercy (feed the hungry, clothe the naked, visit prisons and hospitals, seek out those need) and works of piety (church attendance, Communion, prayer, Scripture reading, fasting, abstinence). Such "works" were methods that recalled Wesley's days at Oxford when the Holy Club's strict style of living earned it the term "Methodist."

Parishioner 2 felt that the leadership should bring professional ministers with correctional experiences to train and equip other leaders and the laity round the issues.

Parishioner 2 responded:

The United Methodist Church should bring in professional ministers from within the correctional institution or someone within the church that is skilled at this level to conduct trainings and workshops on effective reentry practices. Individuals should be trained in conducting worship services, interviewing techniques, life skills, post-prison pastoral counseling follow-up. Moreover, the leadership of the church should follow up with local pastors to ensure that they are being sufficiently trained in this area on an ongoing basis as a requirement to be appointed and/or reappointed back into a parish.

Parishioners 1, 2, and 3 all support prison reentry ministry as a mandate for the United Methodist Church and reminded us of the scriptural support for assisting those in need, remembering that both the Old and New Testaments point to our purpose in helping those who have been in bondage and oppressed. Parishioner 3 stated the following:

> I think the leaders have a biblical mandate to bring justice to this humanitarian issue. There are countless passages in scripture that points towards justice and liberation of prisoners. The themes of prison justice run throughout the old and new testaments. The role of the church is to bring flesh to God's living word. They must continuously engage not just the church but must also engage the world—and should challenge institutions and systems of power that seek to condemn prisoners to a perpetual cycle of poverty.

Parishioner 4 supported the need for training and for doing it in a formal concerted manner would to keep the vision of the church at the forefront: Parishioner 4 responded as such:

> The role of the leaders of the church in preparing the laity for restorative justice and reentry ministries should be one of facilitation. While training, preparing, and empowering at some point end in the formal since, the leadership should always facilitate a connection to resources and be a keeper of the vision coaxing congregations into line with the overall vision for the particular way it sees restorative justice and reentry programs taking shape.

Parishioner 5 felt that the United Methodist Church should be producing "justice seekers; in this process of restoring people back to a place of dignity. Training and support should be provided to the laity. Parishioner 5 believes that "the UMC should empower its laity to become justice-seekers—in the truest sense of the word. This means that we must give the laity and formerly incarcerated individual's agency to articulate and to create an alternative reality to their plight."

Parishioner 6 felt that more analysis of current needs, problems, successes and weaknesses should be done to ensure that the United Methodist Church has the capacity to take on another massive ministry. While supportive of prison reentry and the Church's role, they noted the following must happen first by the leadership:

> The leadership of the UMC church should do a S.W.A.T. analysis every year as a way to continue to improve on this front. The leadership also needs to be much more diverse in its makeup. The people at the top making the decisions in this area should reflect the diversity of the community/population to which it seeks to serve. We also need to start inviting people with a marked past and who have been fully reconciled to the church onto our prison reentry board at the conference and district level.

Parishioner 7 had a totally different take and felt that when people are arrested they should be able to go the church and testify and get support. The church should, in turn, empower persons through the love of God and His goodness in hopes of changing them and our communities. Parishioner 7 shared "when people are arrested people should be able to testify within the church and to get up in front of the church and to let people know what went wrong, what happened, and ask the church for support. Churches have a lot of power. We need to change the culture of church and to empower people to get in front of their circumstances."

The final Guiding Question focused on the specifics of what churches should be trained to do. All respondents shared their views, presented below.

Question 4: What should churches be trained to do in order to deal with prison reentry and restorative justice programs. Parishioner 1 felt initial training should take place where the prisoners are and work to understand their situation without judgment. Parishioner 1 suggested that a cadre of people be trained to do outreach and assist the prisoner upon reentry.

Parishioner 1 gave an extensive response to *Guiding Question 4*:

> Churches and laity must be trained to go where the prisoners are. Basically, instead of assuming we understand their plight, we must work to build intentional communities. A core group of people should be trained to go into prison populations and to help craft effective outreach programs to help people get their lives back on the right track. This includes interviewing the people, their families, their victims, etc. Churches must also take a step back about the way we think about people in prison and who are being released from prison. Folks must not label people as being inherently "bad" for having had a prison experience. "But for the grace of God, there goes I." Churches should be trained to go into local prisons and work closely with the wardens and prison chaplains—especially with folks who will be released to a geographical region. For example, we should attempt to establish a partnership with the state department of corrections, the local mayor's office, the parole commission, etc. on ways to identify who will be coming back into the community, and begin to work with individuals before, during, and after their release.
>
> Moreover, we must reinvigorate our church by being a praying congregation with a proactive orientation. We should task a group of people/committee and adopt a local prison institution and pray regularly for inmates, their families, their overseers, and their victims.
>
> We must be a welcoming and radically hospitable church. We must minister to released prisoners and their families and accept them into our Christian family; this includes visiting with them often, praying with them, hosting character development training, and teaching and empowering them with the word of God.

We must focus on discipleship— we must work closely with prison chaplains on ways in which a core group of people from SUMC could go into the prison and teach bible study, through our "Incarceration Outreach Ministry."

We must partner with other agencies working in this area— such as the Inside-Out Prison Exchange Program. This program helps us to understand curriculum development, developing institutional relationships, engage with interactive pedagogical approaches, whereby prisoners get to tell us their stories. We must facilitate dialogue across faith and denominational differences.

Parishioner 2 shared that in essence there should be a peer-group created along with spending more time building relationships to deal with issues around race, culture, and denominational differences that tend to divide. Parishioner 2 gave the response below:

The church should work to become accountability partners for recently released prisoners. Basically, the local church should establish a laity-peer mentor relationship with the formerly incarcerated inmate and check in with the person twice a week via phone/ or in person. Churches should also spend time building intentional communities across lines of race, culture, and denominational lines, so that each person's humanity is valued, appreciated, and respected at the highest level regardless to their alleged infraction or sin against society. Lastly, churches and those who work closely with this population must learn how to relate to inmates—and this happens primarily by creating safe space to engage in the art of storytelling.

Parishioners 2 and 3 believed that to some degree, training is needed especially in the areas of diversity and that the Church should not engage in empty feel good types of ministry. Parishioner 3 shared the following response to *Guiding Question 4:*

Churches should engage in ongoing diversity training to deal with the certain populations. Churches should utilize laity that has experience working with this type of population. In other words, we should not engage in "feel good ministry" for the sake of doing something charitable—instead we should use formerly incarcerated persons and other experienced professional to host training workshops/conferences throughout the year.

Parishioner 4 suggested that healthy boundaries and clear cut training in the areas of accountability needed to be in place. Working with local community groups, chambers of commerce, and law enforcement would serve as ideal resources for training and collaboration. Parishioner 4 shared the following responses:

Churches must be trained in how to set healthy boundaries in order to make the transition back into community smoother for the individual as well as members of the community. Congregations should also be involved with their local Chamber of Commerce, and local political representatives to ensure that programming is being funded and provided with consistency and accessibility. They should have overlapping structures of organization that ensure everyone involved understands how to move someone from the beginning of the reentry process through to the end of the process, whatever that may be for the congregation and community.

Parishioner 5 noted that there should be engagement in the political process regarding this issue and that churches must engage the community on a more collective basis through partnership building. Parishioner 5 shared the following response regarding *Guiding Question 4*:

Churches must be trained to engage the political process whether in the local community or at the state or national level. Churches cannot do it alone; they need the help of political leaders and other faith based community organizers and activist. Churches must be creative in trying to attain funding for these programs. This means churches must solicit public support from donors, organizations, social justice institutions, state departments, and other entities that has a keen interest in the development of this area.

Similar to Parishioner 5, Parishioner 6 believed that some of the burden around this issue should be shared with other community agencies and local congregations. Parishioner 5 perceived *Guiding Question 4* with the following response: "Churches should find a way to share the burden with other entities. Local congregations cannot do it on their own. They simply do not have the capacity to do so. Therefore, laity should be trained extensively in the area of outreach, fundraising, and leveraging and connecting resources from within and outside of the church."

Parishioner 7 took a practical approach to this question and felt that churches should focus on rehabilitation of those persons retuning back to the community and to live by *Matthew 25* as it describes the path to God's liberation. Parishioner 7 shared the following response:

> Churches should teach people how to use public transportation, help people make a smooth transition, churches should walk with people. Churches needs to focus on rehabilitation. We need to think differently about incarceration. We have a system of revenge instead of helping people be restored. Churches needs to teach Matthew 25 and live into that. This particular text says that for those who is dispossessed that God is going to liberate you to wholeness. Churches must refer back to the heart of the Gospel and train people to engage in the work of healing communities.

Summary

This chapter laid out the methodology for gathering feedback about the current efforts in prison reentry ministry, as well as the opportunities and obligations that parishioners perceive the Church has moving forward. Across the board, there was strong support for prison ministry and reentry ministry to be a core program of the United Methodist Church. Parishioners participating in the focus groups and individual interviews offered specific ideas about the ways in which church leadership, clergy, and laity can all proclaim the Gospel by ministering to those formerly in prison and helping to reincorporate them into the church and secular communities.

CHAPTER SIX

The Proposed Blueprint for the United Methodist Church:
A Call To Action

Introduction

The purpose of this chapter is to recommend and provide a preliminary blueprint (action plan) based on the 2004 *Mission Plan for Restorative Justice Ministries* (MPRJM) for the United Methodist Church. The blueprint will be informed by this document that was conceived and adopted by the United Methodist Church in 2004 and revised and readopted in 2008 and part of the various resolutions and the Social Principles of the *Book of Resolutions of the United Methodist Church* (Cropsey & Minus, 2012). It must be understood that many churches within the United Methodist organization currently are conducting similar initiatives, but many are not.

This blueprint is meant to affirm, inform, and operationalize the recommendations with action orientated steps and potential timelines for implementation for the United Methodist Church. This measure is important as the church confronts the core issue of mass incarceration, the prison industrial complex, and the vast number of ex-prisoners returning to their communities. Many of these ex-prisoners have no place to go, and lack hope and a sense of true freedom from their previous bondage and oppression within the criminal justice system. The blueprint integrates many of the recommendations at the various levels of the United Methodist Church's 2004 *Mission Plan for Restorative Justice Ministries.*

Early Call to Action of the United Methodist Church

The visionary duty and obligation of the United Methodist Church compelled early conversations from the 1996 General Conference that declared United Methodists are called to do the following:

- Repent of the sin we have committed that has fostered retributive justice.
- Speak prophetically and consistently against dehumanization in the criminal justice systems.
- Establish restorative justice as the theological ground for ministries in The United Methodist Church and build bridges of collaboration and cooperation to advance the practice of restorative justice with boards and agencies within The United Methodist Church, with United Methodist and other Methodist communions around the globe, with other faith communities in the United States and worldwide, and with nonprofit organizations and/or governmental organizations.
- Intensify our redemptive ministries with those who work within criminal justice, victims of crime and their families, those who are incarcerated in jails and prisons and their families, and communities traumatized by crime.

Elements of Successful Prison Reentry Programs

Several researchers have attempted to determine the elements that constitute a successful reentry program for ex-prisoners in the community of faith context (Mears, Roman, Wolff, & Buck, 2006; McRoberts, 2002). The results vary and are hard to pinpoint in terms of which are effective and not effective, especially for programs that have a spiritual or religious orientation to them (Mears, Roman, Wolff, & Buck, 2006).

A publication by Drake and LaFrance (2007) shared the Urban Institute's Justice Policy center, the National Institute of Justice, the National Institute of Corrections and the U.S. Department of Education's Office of Correctional Education's lists of recommendations appropriate to serve ex-offenders upon release from prison in any community context by intermediary agencies:

1 Focus on motivation, envisioning new roles and self-concepts, and nurturing the commitment to change.
2 Provide for a gradual transition from the institutional structure of prison to an open schedule.
3 Offer support and immediate access to income in the days following release.
4 Look for compatibilities between individuals' temperaments and available jobs.
5 Provide non-punitive, problem-solving assistance.
6 Develop resources or provide access to concrete supports like transportation, interview and work clothes, child care, housing and food.
7 Create a well-developed network of potential employers.
8 Cultivate employer satisfaction through frequent contact and willingness to mediate conflicts.
9 Coordinate employment and criminal justice commitments to provide as little disruption to job responsibilities as possible.
10 Focus on job retention.

The Urban Ministry (n.d.) has adopted and suggests the following best practices for ex-offender reentry programs as informed by the work of Gaes, Flanagan, Motiuk, & Stewart (1998):

1 Focus your program on the ex-offenders who are most likely to recidivate.

2 Intervention should be focused on the qualities that are known to place a person at risk to commit crime.

3 Intervention should be comprehensive; that is, it should treat as many needs of participants as possible.

4 Teach the participants to recognize and resist antisocial behavior.

5 Try to discover the learning styles of your program participants and then match them with staff whose teaching styles would best accommodate them.

6 The program should last about 3 to 9 months.

7 Treatment should come from well-funded programs with committed staff.

8 Community-based programs are believed to be more effective than institutionbased programs.

9 Involve a Researcher when designing and developing your program.

According to the Prison Fellowship Ministries Program,[12] successful reentry is best accomplished through a three phased approach, listed below: (Prison Fellowship Ministries)

1 Preparation: Beginning 6 to 12 months prior to release, volunteers focus on equipping the prisoner with skills, education, and resources needed to make a successful transition to the outside world. This usually involves coordination between in-prison ministry volunteers and reentry volunteers. The primary goal is for the prisoner to have a detailed reentry plan in place before the expected release date.

2 Transition: When the ex-prisoner leaves the prison gates, reentry volunteers make sure he or she has safe housing, food, clothing, and many other key supports. During the early days of release, most ex-prisoners need daily encour-

[12] https://www.prisonfellowship.org/resources/training-resources/reentryministry/ministrybasics/phases-of-reentry/.

Dr. Herron Keyon Gaston

agement and assistance until their initial crisis-level needs are resolved.

3 Then they need continued weekly contact, spiritual guidance, and emotional support for 6 to 12 months as they find employment, begin to rebuild relationships, and adapt to their new life.

4 Stabilization: Volunteers continue to disciple and assist the ex-prisoner toward establishing consistent personal habits, healthy relationships, spiritual growth, and church commitment. One very important sign of stabilization is when the ex-prisoner becomes involved in serving others in the community instead of expecting to be served. This phase usually takes 12 to 24 months.

The United Methodist Model

The following represent the recommendations/tasks put forth by the United Methodist Church conference initially in 1996 and in subsequent years (2000, 2004, and 2008) during their General Conference. The information is presented below with groups or units response for carrying them out. Parishioners' responses were categorized under each of the four guiding questions along with the four different levels/areas within the United Methodist Church.

Based on the recommendations of two United Methodist Church District Superintendents, along with myself, during a facilitation workshop around prison ministry for the Connecticut District in March 2017, we concluded based on feedback from parishioners over the past two years who have engaged in prison ministry from two local parishes, that in order for prison ministry to be successful in our current day context, we must focus on "holistic reentry." This involves addressing all areas of concerns for returning citizens. In other words, the United Methodist Church, and other churches and denominations who have a peculiar interest in this work in general, must better address the social, spiritual, intellectual, political, cultural, environmental, familial, and personal challenges this population faces post incarceration. Towards that end, below are a few pragmatic and practical things we can do as a church community to advance the work of reentry. As previously stated, these recommendations came on the heels of a prison ministry workshop in the State of Connecticut in March of 2017. These recommendations were recorded and later transcribed by the researcher as an authentic expression from two key leaders within the United Methodist Church, along with the researcher. For the sake of confidentiality, I will not name them in this official document, but will refer to them as leader one and leader two.

1 Establishing Authentic and Open Connections: When people feel a sense of authentic engagement, they are more inclined to engage in honest dialogue with others, thus allowing the opportunity to get at the heart of one's concerns, challenges, and issues. The work of building connections is not something that should be short term, but should be continuous over six to twelve months depending on the positive development of the returning citizen. (Leader 2)

2 Prison Ministry Must Be Outward Turning Towards Families: In other words, if we take seriously the moral and ethical responsibility we have towards connecting/ restoring familial relationships as a Christian community, then we must help families to stay connected both while in prison and post prison. The church then must address the basic needs of helping to provide food, clothes, shelter, while creating pipelines of access to employment, healthcare, and other social opportunities. (Leader 2)

3 Faith Communities and Christian Fellowship Must Extend Beyond the Four Walls: Simply put, we must meet people where they are. This includes creating alternative church communities outside of traditional church spaces, alternatives that are aimed at fostering and facilitating discussion and connectedness in way that empowers and inspires one to serve one's respective community, as opposed to the idea of being served. (Leader 1)

4 <u>Job Readiness</u>: Preparing formerly incarcerated persons for employment is crucial for helping them realize that they have a chance to set a positive trajectory into the future. We must connect them with apprenticeship programs through United Methodist Church sponsored colleges and universities. This should involve providing formerly incarcerated persons with occupational skills training and on the-job training to reorient them to the workforce, and so that they can make a living wage to take care of themselves and their families. (Leader 2)

5 <u>Building a Safe-Haven and Alternative Community Reality</u>: Churches should advocate being close neighbors to formerly incarcerated persons instead of distant neighbors. In other words, churches should be out front fighting against systemic violence and the various forms of environmental injustices that often plaque communities where the bulk of returning citizens return to live. Churches should empower formerly incarcerated persons to take an active role in their communities by serving on municipal boards that have a broad yet influential impact on the life of the community and its positive transformation. (Leader 1, 2, and Researcher)

Blueprint for Action

In this final section, I will lay out the specific guidelines that the Church, and churches of any denomination, may follow in order to minister to those reentering community and family life after incarceration. This blueprint, along with specific action plans, offers the guidance needed to attend to formerly incarcerated persons' physical, emotional, psychological, and spiritual needs as they leave prison and try to find their way on the outside. The blueprint has grown out of the four guiding questions that have guided this project from the beginning:

1 How can the United Methodist Church play a greater role in assisting with prison reentry and restorative justice?

2 How can the leadership and connectional mission of the United Methodist Church be used to create a blueprint for restorative justice programs through its connectional system?

3 What is the role of the leaders of the United Methodist Church in training, preparing, and empowering its laity for restorative justice and reentry activities within its current structure?

4 What should churches be trained to do in order to deal with prison reentry and restorative justice programs?

In the tables that follow, the Call to Action and Blueprint, the statements listed in the Recommendations/Actions column are the specific action items that can/should be undertaken to create robust, theologically grounded programs for prison reentry ministry throughout the UMC. This list is not complete; it is a beginning that includes tasks and initiatives revealed through the intense work of the Summerfield UMC ministry, as well as the work being undertaken by other prison reentry ministry programs. I have partnered these items with the guiding questions to offer a pathway for addressing the specific concerns of this project. The Responsible Parties column identifies the different individuals and groups/committees within the UMC who I believe are best trained and positioned to facilitate the corresponding Recommendations/Actions.

In the Enhanced Mission Plan – Blueprint/Roadmap, I have used the existing Action lists to create a more holistic approach to creating a program that serves the formerly incarcerated. The Enhanced Mission Plan creates a framework that seeks to identify the global areas of concerns faced y formerly incarcerated person, whereas the Call to Action and Blueprint offers a more general outline of the work to be done. Both sections are essentially a starting point. Further work must be undertaken to expand each of these items more fully to address practical implementation, fund allocation, policies, structure, staffing, etc.

Call to Action and Blueprint: Guiding Question 1

How can the United Methodist Church play a greater role in assisting with prison reentry and restorative justice?

Goal: For the United Methodist Church to play a greater role in assisting with prison reentry and restorative justice initiatives.

Strategy: The General Church

Recommendation/Action	Responsible Parties
— Expand the UMC's Restorative Justice Ministries through the Restorative Justice Ministries Committee.	— The General Conference — Restorative Justice Ministries Committee — Council of Bishops
— Expand the Restorative Justice Ministries	— The General Conference — Restorative Justice Ministries Committee
— Committee to include representatives from: General Board of Global Ministries, Board of Higher Education and Ministry, the General Council on Ministries and the General Commission on Religion and Race, United Methodist Women, United Methodist Men, and 7 at-large selected by the Council of Bishops.	— Council of Bishops
— Fund the agency to conduct its work.	— General Board of Global Ministries — Board of Higher Education and Ministry, — The General Council on Ministries — The General Commission on Religion and Race — United Methodist Women, United Methodist Men, and 7 at-large selected by the Council of Bishops

— Ensure a biblical/theological foundation for a restorative justice approach to criminal justice.	— The General Conference — Restorative Justice Ministries Committee
— Become a center for networking, teaching, learning, and networking.	— The General Conference — Restorative Justice Ministries Committee
— Work collegially with other groups and organizations whether they are inside or outside the denomination, religious or secular, to find common ground to bring about systemic change in the spirit of mediation (even when there is disagreement about theological rationale).	— The General Conference — Restorative Justice Ministries Committee
— Coordinate training, networking, and advocacy for UMC Restorative Justice Ministries by working with jurisdictions, annual conferences, central conferences, districts, local United Methodist churches and their communities.	— The General Conference — Restorative Justice Ministries Committee
— Serve as the primary advocate and interpreter of Restorative Justice Ministries.	— The General Conference — Restorative Justice Ministries Committee
— Identify and expand critical models and facilitate the development of Restorative Justice Ministries, on a global basis, at all levels of The United Methodist Church.	— The General Conference — Restorative Justice Ministries Committee

Call to Action and Blueprint: Guiding Question 2

How can the leadership and connectional mission of the United Methodist Church be used to create a blueprint for restorative justice programs through its connectional system?

Goal: Mobilize the leadership and connectional mission and structure of the United Methodist Church to place the restorative justice programs at the forefront of its mission.

Strategy: Specific General Church Agencies

Recommendation/Action	Responsible Parties
— Restorative Justice Ministries Committee provides guidance and oversight to the operation of the Restorative Justice Ministries with each board/agency providing the funds to continue the work of Restorative Ministries to meet mandates and initiatives.	— General Board of Global Ministries
— General Board of Global Ministries provides resources to annual and central conferences to enable them to develop Restorative Justice Ministries with victims, offenders, prisoners, their families, and communities.	— General Board of Global Ministries
— General Board of Global Ministries provides funding to support gatherings of United Methodists working in the fields of criminal justice, community corrections, and restorative justice. The events will focus on the relationship between faith and work.	— General Board of Global Ministries

— General Board of Global Ministries provides funding to organize global consultations on restorative justice to be held in central conferences, bringing together United Methodist leaders from across the globe who are using restorative justice ministry strategies and techniques to transform and resolve social, political, religious, economic, racial, and ethnic conflicts and end violence within their churches and communities.	— General Board of Global Ministries
— General Board of Global Ministries works with annual and central conferences and their ecumenical, interfaith, and community partners to develop victim offender reconciliation programs and neighborhood conflict resolution programs based on restorative justice ministries models to serve the church and community.	— General Board of Global Ministries
— General Board of Global Ministries, in consultation with annual and central conferences, organizes training events in restorative justice ministries.	— General Board of Global Ministries
— General Board of Global Ministries evaluates and identifies model programs of restorative justice ministries and develops the network for these ministries.	— General Board of Global Ministries

Dr. Herron Keyon Gaston

— General Board of Global Ministries works with the boards and agencies to develop written resources to assist the church in their work in these ministries.	— General Board of Global Ministries
— General Board of Global Ministries works with the Disciple Bible Study Ministries in order to increase the involvement of annual conferences and local congregations in ministries with prisoners, ex-offenders and juvenile offenders.	— General Board of Global Ministries — Disciple Bible Study Ministries
— General Board of Global Ministries develops a group of United Methodist trained mediators who can respond to conflicts in the community and who can assist in training other United Methodists to serve as mediators in their communities.	— General Board of Global Ministries
— General Board of Global Ministries develops electronic resources and quarterly newsletters to provide information and updates on new developments in restorative justice ministries around the world served by the UMC.	— General Board of Global Ministries
— General Board of Church and Society advocates for social and economic justice in order to restore and strengthen communities.	— General Board of Church and Society

— General Board of Church and Society advocates for a criminal justice system that is not racist, less costly, more humane, effectively rehabilitative, and accessible to family members of victims and offenders.	— General Board of Church and Society
— General Board of Church and Society provides training and resources to annual and central conferences and local churches advocating for a more just system of justice.	— General Board of Church and Society
— General Board of Church and Society advocates for the abolition of the death penalty worldwide.	— General Board of Church and Society
— General Board of Discipleship develops print and training resources, including Sunday school resources, for local churches to use as they embrace restorative justice ministries. This directive includes: the development of resources and training for reconciling parents and youth offenders; the development of small group resources that support victim and offender reconciliation; and the provision of material for small groups that wish to explore restorative justice issues within the local church.	— General Board of Discipleship
— General Board of Discipleship develops a training and certification process for laity and local church pastors carrying out restorative justice ministries.	— General Board of Discipleship

Dr. Herron Keyon Gaston

— General Board of Higher Education and Ministry provides certification for chaplains and explores the development of certification for others interested in professional ministry with restorative justice ministries.	— General Board of Higher Education and Ministry
— United Methodist Women continue to start units within jails and prisons to promote restorative justice	— United Methodist Women
— United Methodist Women continue ministries with families of prisoners.	— United Methodist Women
— United Methodist Men work jointly with the General Board of Church and Society to resource UMM to become involved in the various aspects of Restorative Justice.	— United Methodist Men — General Board of Church and Society
— United Methodist Women and United Methodist Men consider working with Disciple Bible Study Ministries, KAIROS, and other Bible studies/retreats to start units of Christian disciple making with prisoners, ex-offenders and juvenile offenders.	— United Methodist Women — United Methodist Men — General Board of Church and Society — KAIROS

Call to Action and Blueprint: Guiding Question 3

What is the role of the leaders of the United Methodist Church in training, preparing, and empowering its Laity for restorative justice and reentry activities within its current structure?

Goal: For the United Methodist Church to play a greater role in assisting with prison reentry and restorative justice initiatives.

Strategy: Jurisdictional/Central Conference and Annual Conferences

Recommendation/Action	Responsible Parties
— Support jurisdictional/central conference and annual conference networking as modeled by the Southeastern Jurisdiction's and South Central Jurisdiction's Restorative Justice Network Group.	— Jurisdictional Restorative Justice Network Group
— Bring together clusters of contiguous conferences to expedite processes of training and resource sharing.	— Jurisdictional Restorative Justice Network Group
— Encourage conferences to establish interagency restorative justice task forces to coordinate Restorative Justice Ministries within their bounds, with special emphasis on partnership with the Restorative Justice Ministries Interagency Task Force and the facilitation and resourcing of local church ministries.	— Restorative Justice Ministries Interagency Task Force

Call to Action and Blueprint: Guiding Question 4

What should churches be trained to do in order to deal with prison reentry and restorative justice programs?

Goal: For the United Methodist Church to play a greater role in assisting with prison reentry and restorative justice initiatives.

Strategy: Local Church

Recommendation/Action	Responsible Parties
— Provide adult and youth education programs on restorative justice (theory, practice, issues, models), and use of resources (utilizing curriculum resources, printed and audiovisual, provided through connectional sources).	— Local Congregations and Clergy
— Provide safe space to enable people to share real experiences of victimization, incarceration, or other direct encounters with the criminal justice system and/or restorative justice processes.	— Local Congregations and Clergy
— Schedule a "Restorative Justice Ministries Sunday" to generate deeper awareness by the entire congregation regarding the contrasting paradigms of retributive justice and restorative justice and their different goals and outcomes.	— Local Congregations and Clergy
— Organize or form direct service and/or advocacy efforts to support the work of restorative justice; and work with local ecumenical and/or interfaith agencies and other community agencies.	— Local Congregations and Clergy

— Convene representatives of the restorative justice community to define policy/legislative needs and strategies.	— Local Congregations and Clergy
— Encourage/resource congregations to work on restorative justice through regional judicatories and media.	— Local Congregations and Clergy
— Encourage/initiate dialogue with correctional/criminal justice system officials.	— Local Congregations and Clergy
— Identify and nurture relationships with criminal justice system leaders (e.g., judges, attorneys, wardens, police, etc.) to increase awareness of and education about restorative justice.	— Local Congregations and Clergy
— Involve local congregations in ministries with juvenile detention centers and domestic violence centers.	— Local Congregations and Clergy
— Build covenant discipleship groups at the local level for restorative justice advocates, as well as for other persons involved in the criminal justice system.	— Local Congregations and Clergy
— Provide victim-offender mediation and other restorative justice processes.	— Local Congregations and Clergy
— Identify and develop coalition partnerships with victim assistance groups, advocacy groups, jail and prison ministry groups, and exoffender assistance groups.	— Local Congregations and Clergy
— Plan and implement strategies for advocacy that encourage legislative support for restorative justice programs.	— Local Congregations and Clergy

Dr. Herron Keyon Gaston

The Enhanced Mission Plan – Blueprint/Roadmap

The information below is intended to serve as an effective Roadmap to Reentry which leads towards restorative justice. The purpose of this Roadmap is to identify six key evidence-based best practices that parishioners and key leaders within the United Methodist Church have identified as being mission critical to the work of reentry. Based on the responses from parishioners and leaders from within the United Methodist Church around this project, successful reentry begins 6-12 months _before_ one's initial release from prison. And, just as important, the Church's involvement in reentry must be continuous, comprehensive, and wide-ranging. As such, we must support formerly incarcerated persons through the general phases listed below to ensure a smoother transition back into the community and to address the issue of recidivism. I propose the following areas of focus for a phased approach to a holistic ministry: Education, Housing, Family, Employment, Healthcare, and Spirituality.

EDUCATION 6-12 months prior to release	Churches should work with prison staff to identify educational opportunities on the outside, and to help with college/vocational/apprenticeship admissions process. A personalized reentry plan should be established to address needs based on social, economic, environmental, and educational factors.
HOUSING upon release	Churches should work collaboratively with the local housing authority and other community partners to identify affordable housing opportunities for formerly incarcerated persons. The UMC, in particular, should invest in transitional housing and allow formerly incarcerated persons to live onsite for a period of 60-90 days until they are able to transition on their own.

FAMILY prior to and after release	Churches should work closely with family members of the incarcerated person while in prison and after the prison experience to establish and solidify familial support, so that they do not feel alone. Churches should also assist in meeting the basic necessities of former inmates: food, clothes, shelter, along with other related financial assistance.
EMPLOYMENT prior to release	Conduct an assessment to determine which skills can translate into the workplace. The role of the church is to help to prepare individuals for job readiness by facilitating and hosting workshops, employment training, interviewing skills, etc. as a way to expose individuals to employment resources and to put them on the path to solidifying a competitive career.
HEALTHCARE	In order for formerly incarcerated individuals to be productive members of society and go to work, they need to have access to preventative care for themselves and their families. The role of the church is to help plug them into social service programs, and to educate them about their options.
SPIRITUALITY	Churches should work with formerly incarcerated persons to help them develop a healthy spiritual life that points towards character development, emphasizing self-care and discernment, which in turn encourages one to greater compassion toward others.

Implications for Research and Ministerial Practice

This project provided the framework to deepen the Church's theological understanding of its role in prison ministries of all kinds (during and post incarceration) and to further understand its purpose for humanity as inspired by God's Word. Additionally, the project presented an opportunity to encourage churches in general and the United Methodist Church specifically to engage in meaningful research to gain a greater understanding of the needs, issues, and life factors that position people to enter the system and to prepare them for exit. There is no consistent model and the Church needs more study in this area to understand its role and duty to support this underserved and risky population. Lastly, the project prompted the awareness of the relationship between theology and the broader role of the clergy and how they interact with, minister to, and do their local mission work for this population.

The task, need, and role of prison ministry during the prison stay and after release remains a major critical issue for all U.S. institutions for a variety of reasons. While many institutions deal with the cost and impact of the criminal justice system through the warehousing of inmates for a host of crimes to society and victims; there is no defined approach to solving this problem as a social or public health issue. Moreover, there is no formal and consistent approach to reforming, redeeming, and restoring these same individuals, or even their families, back to the community, or to God by the faith community from a spiritual standpoint. The Church has a clear mandate to "save souls" and to deliver the down-trodden, the poor, the destitute, and the less fortunate from harm to a state of safety in the name of God, the Son of God, and the Holy Spirit. Yet, the Church has systematically fallen short of this mandate. The United Methodist Church has shown great promise and position within the faith community as a denomination historically rooted in the causes of reformation, redemption, and restoration and, therefore, can be a dynamic force in prison ministry during one's prison sentence and after release.

This project presents several major implications for the role of theology, future research, and ministerial practice within the Christian faith and particularly within the United Methodist Church. The results of this study highlighted the need to revisit the role of the Church in supporting the prison reentry ministries, restorative justice, and support. Additionally, the project brought to the forefront several issues around the true mandate of the Church in general and the United Methodist Church in specific.

Implications for Theology

In the tradition of John Wesley, we learned earlier that the theological components of the Methodist movement consist of *Scripture, Tradition, Experience, and Reason,* and therefore this study prompted revisiting these components as necessary ingredients for our "God-thought," ministry, ministers, and for the laity. These ideas of Wesley's have been also referred to as the Wesleyan Quadrilateral (McDargh, 2010, p.3). This project created the opportunity to revisit the four components as we encounter our role as leaders of the Church and within the United Methodist Church to ensure that we understand clearly God's purpose, trusting that when we believe in God and adhere to His Word, we become able and motivated to assist in the healing and restoration of all people, especially those who have committed crimes and other human transgressions and find themselves incarcerated. We have talked a great deal about the statistical data that continue to show an uptick in the number of persons entering our nations' jails and prisons and that the U. S. has the highest incarceration rates of all the developed countries in the world. No longer can the Church think that prisons are places of spiritual or moral rehabilitation when we outpace the world in our prison populations and the number of those who continue to be broken before and after their release.

Like, Pounder (2008), we are obligated to embrace the theology of liberation, hope, and justice, and use all of our power and resources to help people reintegrate back into society and live with the comforts of God's redemptive love. Consistent with this theological thought is the work of Marshall (2002), which supports the role of churches in fostering a restorative sprit and style of supporting and reintegrating ex-prisoners back into the community. This project revealed how parishioners' responses to the *Guiding Questions* made reference to the duty, mandate, or role of the Church as being that force called to help humanity in His name. While the focus of this project was not necessarily focused on race/ethnicity, we understand that God's Word and loving sprit and grace can be transferred and open to all people of all walks of life, cultures, races, and orientations. The Church in general and the United Methodist Church must continue to embrace and expand God's mandate and to continue to reflect, illuminate, and encourage the use of the scripture, tradition, experience, and reason when we encounter opportunities to transform the lives of those who are lost or broken in Christ.

In the wake of theological ideas about prison ministry, I caution church leaders, researchers, and the general church to "apply a ministry model that is faithful to the Father, expressed itself in love for the Son, and is fueled by the power of the Holy Spirit" (Charles, 1993, p.57). Charles (1993) noted that this type of model is fundamentally rooted in the "redemptive reality of the cross, and it avoids the temptations to dissolve the tensions between imminence and transcendence, holiness and love, freedom and responsibility, dignity and depravity" (p.57).

Implications for Research
There are several implications from this project that pose challenges for the research community on the topic of the role of the Church in prison ministry and similar ministries focused on reentry. Due to the variety and historical independence of many church congregations and denominations operating in Christian silos, very little consistent and large-scale research exists nationally about the role, impact, or mandates of the Church around this topic. Therefore, this is an open field of research especially as people begin to accept and expect more accountability, and as there are more public and private collaborations in solving human problems. It is expected that as the prison industrial complex expands and more people enter and exit the prison system it will become incumbent upon all sectors of the community to investigate more closely this phenomena and begin to practice what they preach.

Future research should explore how denominational approaches, techniques, and methods differ, and evaluate the efficacy of prison ministry (during or after). Additionally, more research focusing on how different types of crimes, criminals, and after-care, aids the prisoner upon exit to integrate more smoothly into the community with or without the faith community.

Certainly, more qualitative or mixed-methodologies research would help support more controlled, consistent, and respected research in this area. The use of pre-post techniques, controlled groups, and larger scale representative samples might yield a wealth of information about the efficacy of these faith programs and the impact the Church is making on the successful recovery and reintegration back into the community. Results of such designs and outcomes can inform the scientific research community, as well as those endeavoring to restore persons back to the community and ensure that recidivism is reduced.

Lastly, this project revealed that even among various Christian denominations, many may not understand their role in helping to reform, redeem, and restore people as Christ has done for humanity; and as He requires of us. More research in this area would prove to be important and useful in teaching and preparing Christians to reunite, to become reinvigorated in their own Christian calling by Christ for us all.

Implications for Ministerial Practice

Overall, this project illuminated the role and practice of restorative prison ministry within the Church and within the context of the community. The practice of ministering and providing spiritual nourishment in the wake of a vast prison system and the unprepared ex-prisoners upon exit ought to be on lips of every minister in general and particularly within the United Methodist Church. As one of the parishioners in this project stated:

> I think the leaders have a biblical mandate to bring justice to this humanitarian issue. There are countless passages in scripture that point towards justice and liberation of prisoners. The themes of prison justice run throughout the Old and New Testaments. The role of the church is to bring flesh to God's living word. They must continuously engage not just the Church but must also engage the world—and should challenge institutions and systems of power that seek to condemn prisoners to a perpetual cycle of poverty."

Dr. Herron Keyon Gaston

Clergy must explore those scriptures and make them real in our modern times. I believe Ecclesiastes 9:1 best states the context of the lack of newness of things in the world: "The thing that hath been, it is that which shall be; and that which is done is that which shall be done: and there is no new thing under the sun."

This lack of newness is demonstrated in US prisons and punitive systems of penalty, which are nothing new. Nor is the Christian response to it. Christ as our model of the one who was arrested, detained, tortured, crucified, and rose again should be all the credence needed to ensure that we engage our congregations regularly and remind them that our own liberty and freedom are at stake whether, imprisoned or not, when we do not do God's Will.

For the United Methodist Church congregations, clergy should already be aware of the goals and recommendations of the Mission Plan for Restorative Justice Ministries (MPRJM) and therefore, involved in the practice of carrying out the adopted recommendations of the United Methodist Church and throughout its connectional system. Clergy should ensure that the mandate of God to take care of the sick, feed the poor, and provide shelter to those who are homeless extends generally to all in humanity who are broken and lost. This is a great expectation of the Church in general, but more so a major goal of the United Methodist Church due to its tradition and historical underpinnings of reformation, redemption, and restoration.

Summary and Conclusions

The results of this project offered many contributions to the field of ministry and have many implications for theology, research, and in the practice of restoring those who have been imprisoned. Often philosophical or theoretical theology undergoes a shift when individuals and communities try to implement religion in a practical way. We have come to understand that these are separate dimensions that Christians confuse when doing their mission work. Prison reentry mission work and the like are no exceptions to this type of confusion. This project was important in delineating the differences between theoretical theology and faith in practice; and demonstrating how parishioners and church leaders perceive their roles in restorative justice and the liberation of humanity, locally and abroad. The efforts and energies of the United Methodist Church must be realigned and focused on the recommendations of the Mission Plan for Restorative Justice Ministries (MPRJM) as informed by the current responses of the parishioners in this study and the Blueprint for more directed action. The United Methodist Church is poised to be the leader nationally and internationally in this area of humanity and must adhere to and carry out its mission as reformer, redeemer, and restorer.

APPENDIX A

This appendix provides a historical overview of Summerfield and its long-time commitment to prison fellowship and, in particular, prison reentry initiative. It reflects parishioners' responses to the four guiding questions for parishioners following a focus group, and individual interview responses to determine what parishioners thought in relationship to the role of the United Methodist Church in prison reentry, its role, and spiritual commitment.

Guiding Questions for the Call to Action

1 How can the United Methodist Church play a greater role in assisting with prison reentry and restorative justice?
2 How can the leadership and connectional mission of the United Methodist Church be used to create a blueprint for restorative justice programs through its connectional system?
3 What is the role of the leaders of the United Methodist Church in training, preparing, and empowering its laity for restorative justice and reentry activities within its current structure?
4 What should churches be trained to do in order to deal with prison reentry and restorative justice programs?

Parishioner Responses

Parishioner #1:

Question 1: The United Methodist Church can play an even greater role with prison reentry by focusing more squarely on developing closer relationships with other local congregations (outside of the UMC connectional system) in addressing the needs of the formerly incarcerated population. This way we will be able to address multiple facets of prison ministry within the context of a vast church community. In other words, we need to better connect and pool our resources with other organizations/agencies/partners within local neighborhoods and work alongside the ongoing work in the community in which our local churches sit, as a way to identify assets in the community to reintegrate successfully formerly incarcerated inmates.

Question 2: The UMC boasts having a large number of prison chaplains, wardens, and other prison reformers. These criminal justice practitioners also hold key leadership positions within their respective local congregations. One way in which the leadership of the UMC can create a model blueprint for restorative justice program is by utilizing our vast amount of human re-sources. It would be great to propose as an idea at General Conference to create a "prison reentry think-tank," comprised of correctional professionals, law enforcement, wardens, parole officers, probation officers, and other criminal justice players to collaborate under one roof and to brainstorm about ways to create an alternate reality for prisoners. At present, the UMC is in a good position to lead the "faith based reentry" charge because of its ecclesial commitment to protecting and standing against all forms of injustice as we endeavor to create holistic healing communities with an aim to set the captives free and to restore them spiritually back to wholeness.

Question 3: Leaders within the UMC have a moral and ethical obligation to speak truth to power and to challenge systems of dominance with bold pro-clivity. Rooted in a prophetic tradition of isolating and challenging what is understood to be deeply flawed and morally defective is paramount to un-derstanding the character of the UMC. The role of leaders in the UMC are to be "moral agitators" committed to justice. Moreover, the role of the church is to create compassionate ministries that equip the laity and other faith leaders within the church to work within and outside the church and to truly be God's hands and feet to the world. Local clergy should be in the business of equipping leaders with knowledge of the Bible around our shared/individual obligation as moral agents to pursue and to seek God's justice. It is incumbent upon us to foster and forge healing communities, thus providing an intimate setting necessary for spiritual growth. Hence, the ethos of the UMC is that God is in close solidarity and identification with the wounded, sick, poor, and imprisoned; that what is done to them is done to God (Matt. 25:31-46). At the heart of God's nature is reconciliation. God was in Christ reconciling the world unto Godself and calling the church as an agent of reconciliation (II Cor. 5:1621)

"I shall endeavor to show," said John Wesley, "that Christianity is essentially a social religion, and that to turn it into a solitary one is to destroy it." With characteristic directness he then spelled out for his followers the specific methods they could employ to avoid this dangerous pitfall of solitariness. In the General Rules of 1743, he Methodists to practice works of mercy (feed the hungry, clothe the naked, visit prisons and hospitals, seek out those in need) and works of piety (church attendance, Communion, prayer, Scripture reading, fasting, abstinence). Such "works" were methods that recalled Wesley's days at Oxford when the Holy Club's strict style of living earned it the term "Methodist."

Question 4: Churches, including the laity, must be trained to go where the prisoners are. Basically, instead of assuming we understand their plight, we must work to build intentional communities. A core group of people should be trained to go into prison populations and to help craft effective outreach programs to help people get their lives back on the right track. This includes interviewing the people, their families, their victims, etc.. Churches must also take a step back about the way we think about people in prison and who are being released from prison. Folks must not label people as being inherently "bad" for having had a prison experience. "But for the grace of God, there go I." Churches should be trained to go into local prisons and work closely with the wardens and prison chaplains, especially with folks who will be released to a geographical region. For example, we should attempt to establish a partnership with the state department of corrections, the local mayor's office, the parole commission, etc., on ways to identify who will be coming back into the community, and begin to work with individuals before, during, and after their release.

Moreover, we must reinvigorate our church by being a praying congregation with a proactive orientation. We should task a group of people/committee and adopt a local prison institution and pray regularly for inmates, their families, their overseers, and their victims. We must be a welcoming and radically hospitable church. We must minister to released prisoners and their families and accept them into our Christian family; this includes visiting with them often, praying with them, hosting character development training, and teaching and empowering them with the word of God. We must focus on discipleship. We must work closely with prison chaplains on ways in which a core group of people from SUMC could go into the prison and teach bible study, through our "Incarceration Outreach Ministry." We must partner with other agencies working in this area, such as the Inside-Out Prison Exchange Program. This program helps us to understand curriculum development, develop institutional relationships, and engage with interactive pedagogical approaches, whereby prisoners get to tell us their stories. We must facilitate dialogue across faith and denominational differences.

Parishioner #2:

Question 1: The UMC should create a uniform reentry program that focuses keenly on programs that address the needs of prison inmates upon being released. I think each parish should create a space or a center that gives former inmates a place to live, grow, and develop in their faith while providing them with opportunities to find a job, transportation to and from work, along with a secure place to live and assisting them with the job search process. We need to help people to feel self-reliant, to become productive citizens of society who have something to offer their respective communities, their families, and themselves.

Dr. Herron Keyon Gaston

Question 2: The United Methodist Church is devoted and committed from an ecclesial perspective and its foundational beliefs to the idea that prisoners are an integral part of God's beloved community. This general ethos of the institutional church's mission speaks to the character and personality of the UMC on the whole. The UMC already has a target population (men, women, children, juveniles, and families). We already have skilled and talented men and women within our ranks who have done this type of work over the span of their careers. We have eager volunteers to help assist in this area of the church's adopted mission.

Question 3: The United Methodist Church should bring in professional ministers from within the correctional institution or others within the church, who are skilled to conduct trainings and workshops on effective reentry practices. Individuals should be trained in conducting worship services, interviewing techniques, life skills, and post-prison pastoral counseling follow-up. Moreover, the leadership of the church should follow up with local pastors to ensure that they are being sufficiently trained on an ongoing basis as a requirement to be appointed and/or reappointed to a parish.

Question 4: The church should work to become accountability partners for recently released prisoners. The local church should establish a laity-peer mentor relationship with the formerly incarcerated inmate and check in with the person twice a week via phone or in person. Churches should also spend time building intentional communities across lines of race, culture, and denominational lines so that each person's humanity is valued, appreciated, and respected at the highest level regardless to their alleged infraction or sin against society. Lastly, churches and those who work closely with this population must learn how to relate to inmates — and this happens primarily by creating safe space to engage in the art of storytelling.

Parishioner #3:
Question 1: The UMC must learn to work more collaboratively with other institutions, organizations, and ministries that are already doing this work

and are producing tangible results. I think whenever we work on something as large as the prison issue, we need all hands on deck. Besides, each faith community looks differently and the needs are all different. There is no one-size-fits-all. The UMC could afford to be more proactive than reactive when it comes to reentry initiatives. We need to continuously send our leadership to training, and the leadership needs to share that training or educational experience in the local church. The leadership of the church should not just arm local clergy with handling this complex aspect of ministry, but leaders themselves should get at eye-level with this population, as well, by engaging more on the ground instead of brainstorming in the ivory tower or some lofty conference room space in a distant hotel.

Question 2: The UMC has tons of resources within the connectional system. Local clergy should be required to attend at least one/two trainings in this area a year, regardless of the individual mission of their local parish. In 2012, there were more UMC clergy/laity working in the White House Faith Based Office than folks represented from other denominations. Therefore, the UMC is in a unique position to lead the conversation on how to engage this very complex issue the best.

Question 3: I think the leaders have a biblical mandate to bring justice to this humanitarian issue. There are countless passages in scripture that points towards justice and liberation of prisoners. The themes of prison justice run throughout the old and new testaments. The role of the church is to bring flesh to God's living Word. They must continuously engage not just the church, but also the world — and should challenge institutions and systems of power that seek to condemn prisoners to a perpetual cycle of poverty.

Question 4: Churches should engage in ongoing diversity training to deal with certain populations. Churches should utilize laity who have experience working with this type of population. In other words, we should not engage in "feel good ministry" for the sake of doing something charitable. Instead, we should use formerly incarcerated persons and other experienced professionals to host training workshops/conferences throughout the year.

Parishioner #4:

Question 1: At the forefront of any reentry programs must be meaningful connections with the business community, such that the end of reentry programs is employability. Such that the end is reconciliation, the Church must see reentry ministry as a central part of its ministry, bringing people into reconciliation with one another, and by that, greater reconciliation with God. Practically this looks like a leveraging Church investment on a national level toward enticing business owners to hire formerly incarcerated persons and establishing our congregations as Accessible and Affirming spaces for them.

Question 2: On a funding level the connectional structure of the Church can lend itself toward innovative funding ideas, particularly as we explore where to focus our missional spending. Moreover, it has the possibility of pushing us toward rethinking how congregations interact intra-communally toward the planning of events and coordinating of resources to assist in fostering restorative justice locally. It may also provide an opportunity for Churches without pastors or with dwindling memberships to see new ministry opportunities in connection with their sister congregations toward a realization of Christ's beloved community.

Question 3: The role of the leaders of the church in preparing the laity for restorative justice and reentry ministries should be one of facilitation. While training, preparing, and empowering at some point end in the formal sense, the leadership should always facilitate a connection to resources and be a keeper of the vision coaxing congregations into line with the overall vision for the particular way it sees restorative justice and reentry programs taking shape.

Question 4: Churches must be trained in how to set healthy boundaries in order to make the transition back into community smoother for the individual as well as members of the community. Congregations should also be involved with the local Chamber of Commerce, and local political representatives to ensure that programming is being funded and provided with consistency and accessibility. They should have overlapping structures of organization that ensure everyone involved understands how to move someone from the beginning of the reentry process through to the end of the process, whatever that may be for the congregation and community.

Parishioner #5

Question 1: The United Methodist Church should create a public policy "think tank" that works very closely with state, local, and national leaders in implementing smart, common sense legislation to help create diversion programs that will put people back to work and reorient them into the life of their respective communities.

Question 2: The UMC should spend more resources in this area as opposed to focusing on issues outside of the US context. This means that we need to redirect our priorities to address this crucial aspect of ministry that many in our urban churches are facing. This is also an issue for those living in our suburban communities, as many of our constituents either work for a correctional facility, or have one in their backyard. In other words, all of us are complicit and culpable either directly or indirectly in this issue of mass incarceration.

Question 3: The UMC should empower its laity to become justice-seekers, in the truest sense of the word. This means that we must give the laity and formerly incarcerated individuals the agency to articulate and to create an alternative reality to their plight.

Question 4: Churches must be trained to engage the political process whether in the local community or at the state or national level. Churches cannot do it alone; they need the help of political leaders and other faith based community organizers and activist. Churches must be creative in trying to attain funding for these programs. This means churches must solicit public support from donors, organizations, social justice institutions, state departments, and other entities that have a keen interest in the development of this area.

Dr. Herron Keyon Gaston

Parishioner # 6

Question 1: The United Methodist Church should work closely to identify corporations and businesses who will hire ex-prisoners upon their release within the community. The UMC must also work with local community colleges to offer ex-prisoners a vocation or a certificate program that will allow them to compete in the job market. They must also go outside of the local church and pair with other organizations working towards a similar goal. It makes no sense to reinvent the wheel.

Question 2: Smaller churches with large endowments should think about merging with other churches that are doing the practical work of ministry. We must find creative ways to pool our resources together to ensure that they are going to good use, instead of just holding the doors of a church open and the ministry is ineffective.

Question 3: The leadership of the UMC should do a swat analysis every year as a way to continue to improve on this front. The leadership also needs to be much more diverse in its makeup. The people at the top making the decisions in this area should reflect the diversity of the community/population which it seeks to serve. We also need to start inviting people with a marked past and who have been fully reconciled to the church onto our prison reentry board at the conference and district level.

Question 4: Churches should find a way to share the burden with other entities. Local congregations cannot do it on their own. They simply do not have the capacity to do so. Therefore, laity should be trained extensively in the area of outreach, fundraising, and leveraging and connecting resources from within and outside of the church.

Parishioner # 7

Question 1: The United Methodist Church should help them with transitioning. They need to teach people how to use the cell phone, the internet, and other technological advancements. Churches must work to reduce recidivism. We need to value people and create strong relationships. We must help people to think differently and must put people to work.

Question 3: When people are arrested they should be able to testify within the church and to get up in front of the church and let people know what went wrong, what happened, and ask the church for support. Churches have a lot of power. We need to change the culture of church to empower people to get in front of their circumstances.

Question 4: Churches should teach people how to use public transportation, help people make a smooth transition, churches should walk with people. Churches need to focus on rehabilitation. We need to think differently about incarceration. We have a system of revenge instead of helping people be restored. Churches need to teach Matthew 25 and live into that. This particular text says that for those who are dispossessed that God is going to liberate you to wholeness. Churches must refer back to the heart of the Gospel and train people to engage in the work of healing communities.

Parishioner #8
Question 1: The UMC should address mass incarceration by helping to identify people within our connectional church that have been incarcerated and provide them with an opportunity to come forward, and to give the church a visual reminder that this is a central reality and at the heart of the church. We need to reframe mass incarceration from being seen as an issue to a personal experience. Basically, we must demonstrate how real people's lives are affected by this issue. Churches must get passed shame and discuss the rawness of the issue.

Parishioner #9:
Question 1: The UMC needs to redirect its focus to educate ex-cons in the area of literacy and provide them with life skills. Many ex-offenders must learn interviewing skills, people skills, and other soft skills such as how to

use the internet, balance a checkbook etc.. They also need to learn how to shop for groceries and other relevant household appliances. The church can play a greater role in helping to connect exoffenders to resources in the broader community. The laity and volunteers need to learn to listen to the stories, problems, plights, and challenges that many ex-offenders face and attempt to find solutions for their issues.

REFERENCES

Alexander, M. (2010). *The new Jim Crow: Mass incarceration in the age of color-blindness.* New York: The New York Press.

American Baptist Home Mission Society. (2007-18). Organizational website. http://abhms.org/about-us/

Anderson, R. S. (1979). A Theology for Ministry. In *Theological Foundations for Ministry.* Grand Rapids: Erdmans.

Biggs, B. S. (2009). Solitary Confinement: A Brief History. *Mother Jones.* Retrieved from http://www.motherjones.com/politics/2009/03/solitary-confinement-brief-naturalhistory

Binswanger, I. A., Stern, M. F., Deyo, R. A., Heagerty, P. J., Cheadle, A., Elmore, J. G., & Koepsell, T. D. (2007). Release from Prison: A High Risk of Death for Former Inmates. *The New England Journal of Medicine, 356,* 157-165.

Bonczar, T. (2003). *Prevalence of Imprisonment in the U.S. Population, 1974-2001.* Washington DC: U.S. Department of Justice, Bureau of Justice Statistics.

Brewer, R. M., & Heitzeg, N. A. (2008). The Racialization of Crime and Punishment:

Criminal Justice, Color-blind Racism, and the Political Economy of the Prison Industrial Complex. *American Behavioral Scientist, 51, 5, 625-644.*

Bureau of Justice Statistics (BJS). (2012). *Correctional population in the United States,*

2011. Washington, DC: Bureau of Justice Statistics, Office of Justice Programs, U.S. Department of Justice. Retrieved from http://www.bjs.gov/content/pub/pdf/cpus11.pdf.

Carlson, P. (2016). Luke, the Gospel of Social Justice. *About Catholics.* Retrieved from http://www.aboutcatholics.com/beliefs/luke-the-gospel-of-social-justice/

Cayley, D. (1998). *The Expanding Prison: The Crisis in Crime and Punishment and the Search for Alternatives.* Toronto: Ananasi Press.

Center for Christian Ethics. (2012). Portraits of Prison Ministry. *Christian reflection: A Series in Faith and Ethics.* Waco, TX: Center for Christian Ethics. Retrieved from http://www.baylor.edu/content/services/document.php/163167.pdf

Charles, J. D. (1993). Reflections on Some Theological-Ethical Norms for Prison Ministry: A Response. *The Asbury Theological Journal, 48*(2). Retrieved from http://place.asburyseminary.edu/cgi/viewcontent.cgi?article=1481&context=asburyjournal

Chong, T. (2006). *The I Chong: Meditations from the Joint.* New York: Simon Spotlight Entertainment.

Cleary, R. (2003). The Theory of Social Justice. The Theology of Social Justice. Paper presented at the Anglican Social Responsibilities Network Conference.

Cropsey, M. W., & Minus, C. D. (2012). *The book of resolutions of the United Methodist Church, 2012.* Nashville: United Methodist Publishing.

Drake, E. B., & LaFrance, S. (2007). *Findings on Best Practices of Community Re-Entry Programs for Previously Incarcerated Persons.* San Francisco: LaFrance Associates, LLC. Retrieved from http://www.eisenhowerfoundation.org/docs/ExOffender%20Best%20Practices.pdf

Durose, M. (2014). *Recidivism of Prisoners Released in 30 States in 2005: Patterns from 2005 to 2010. A Special Report.* Washington, DC: U.S. Department of Justice, Office of Justice Programs.

Durose, M., Cooper, A., & Snyder, H. (2014). *Recidivism of Prisoners Released in 30 States in 2005: Patterns from 2005 to 2010 – Update. NCJ 244205.* Washington, DC: Bureau of Justice Statistics, US Department of Justice. https://www.bjs.gov/index.cfm?ty=pbdetail&iid=4986

Feeley, M. & Simon, J. (1992). The New Penology: Notes on the Emerging Strategy of Corrections and Its Implications. *Criminology 30,* 449–474.

Finn, P., & Kuck, S. (2003). *Addressing Probation and Parole Officer Stress: Final Report to the National Institute of Justice.* Washington, DC: U.S. Department of Justice, National Criminal Justice Reference Service. Retrieved from http://www.ncjrs.org/pdffiles1nij/ grants/207012.pdf.

Forman, J. (2012). *Racial Critiques of Mass Incarceration: Beyond the New Jim Crow.* Faculty Scholarship Series, Paper 3599. Retrieved from http://digitalcommons.law.yale.edu/fss_papers/3599

Gaes, G. G., Flanagan, T. J., Motiuk, L., & Stewart, L. (1998). Adult Correctional Treatment. *Crime and Justice, 26,* 361-426.

Garland, D. (2001a). *The Culture of Control: Crime and Social Order in Contemporary Society.* Oxford, England: Clarendon Press.

——. (2001b). *Mass Imprisonment*. London: Sage.

Garlitz, T. (1993). Moral Principles and Foundations for Restorative Justice: A Call for Criminal and Juvenile Justice Reform in Illinois from The Catholic Diocese of Joliet, Peace and Social Justice Ministry. A Working Paper. Retrieved from http://www.paxjoliet.org/advocacy/resjus.html 8/27/2014

——. (1998). Moral Principles and Foundations for Restorative Justice. Retrieved from http://www.ospihm.org/racial-healing/docs/Restorative%20Justice.pdf
Griffith, L. (1993). *The fall of the prison: Biblical perspectives on prison abolition*. Grand Rapids, MI: William B. Eerdmans.

Hall, D. J. (2003). What is Theology? *Cross Currents, 53* (2), 177.

Hansen, K. (2015). *Life After Prison: How the Church Can Help*. Retrieved from http://www.patheos.com/blogs/rhetoricraceandreligion/2015/10/life-after-prison-how-the-church-can-help.html

Hartney, C., & Vuong, L. (2009). *Created Equal: Racial and Ethnic Disparities in the U.S. Criminal Justice System*. Oakland, CA: National Council on Crime and Delinquency.

Hlavka, H., Wheelock, D., & Jones, R. (2015). Exoffender Accounts of Successful Reentry from Prison. *Journal of Offender Rehabilitation, 54 (6)*, 406-428.

Johnson, B. R. (2008). The Faith Factor and Prisoner Reentry. *Interdisciplinary Journal of Research on Religion*. Retrieved from http://www.religjournal.com/pdf/ijrr04005.pdf

Jones, R. (2015). Presbyterians Respond to the Mass Incarceration Crisis: CPJ Training Day Workshop Offers Grassroots Strategies for Change. Retrieved from https://www.pcusa.org/news/2015/3/9/presbyterians-respond-massincarcerationcrisis/

Klaus, B. (2011). Biblical Theology of Ministry. A PowerPoint on the foundations of Biblical theology. Retrieved from https://www.agts.edu/faculty/klaus_BTHB529.html

Koschmann, M. A., & Peterson, B. L. (2013). Rethinking Recidivism: A Communication Approach to Prisoner Reentry. *Journal of Applied Social Sciences, 7* (2), 188-207.

LaFree, G. (1998). *Losing Legitimacy: Street Crime and the Decline of Social Institutions in America*. Boulder, CO: Westview Press.

Langan, P. A., & Levin, D. (2002). *Recidivism of Prisoners Released in 1994, Bureau of Justice Statistics Special Report NCJ 193427*. Washington, DC: U.S. Department of Justice.

Larson-Miller, L. (2015). Rites of Reconciliation and Healing in Christian History. Oxford Research Encyclopedia of Religion. DOI: 10.1093/ acrefore /97801 9934 0378.013.71

Leung, F., & Savithiri, R. (2009). Spotlight on Focus Groups. Hypothesis. *Canadian Family Physician, 55,* 281-219. Retrieved from https://www.ncbi.nlm.nih.gov/pmc/articles/PMC2642503/pdf/0550218.pdf

Love, S. L. (2001). Teaching a Theology of Ministry Based on the Gospels. *Leaven 9 (2),* article 9. Retrieved from https://digitalcommons.pepperdine.edu/cgi/viewcontent.cgi?article=1553&context =leaven.

Lynch, J. P., & Sabol, W. J. (2001). *Prisoner Reentry in Perspective.* Crime Policy Report, 3. Washington, DC: Urban Institute, Justice Policy Center.

Lynch, L. E. (2014, December 12). *National Institute of Justice annual report.* Washington, DC: US Dept of Justice. Retrieved April 25 2018 from https://www.ncjrs.gov/pdffiles1/nij/249533.pdf

Mansell, I., Bennett, G., Northway, R., Mead, D., & Moseley, L. (2004). The Learning Curve: The Advantages and Disadvantages in the Use of Focus Groups as a Method of Data Collection. *Nurse Research, 11* (4), 79-88.

Marshall, C. D. (2002). Prison, Prisoners, and the Bible. Breaking Down the Walls Conference. Retrieved from http://restorativejustice.org/10fulltext/marshallchristopher.-prison-prisoners-and-the-bible.pdf

Martinson, R. (1974). What Works? Questions and Answers About Prison Reform. *The Public Interest.* Retrieved November 21, 2017, from http://www.pbpp.pa.gov/research_statistics/Documents/Martinson-What Works 1974.pdf

Mauer, M. (2006). *Race to Incarcerate.* New York: New Press.

———. (2011). Addressing Racial Disparities in Incarceration. *The Prison Journal, 91* (3), 87S-101S.

McDargh, J. (2010). Called by Our True Names: Theological Reflections on Prison Ministry. Talk at "You Visited Me": The Urgent Challenge of Prison Ministry, October 29, 2010, Boston College School of Theology and Ministry and the Church in the 21st Century. Retrieved from https://www.bc.edu/content/dam/files/top/church21/pdf/PM%20Conference%20McDargh%20Text%20and%20Resources.pdf

McRoberts, O. M. (2002). Religion, Reform, Community: Examining the Idea of

ChurchBased Prisoner Reentry. Talk at Reentry Roundtable Prisoner Reentry and the Institutions of Civil Society: Bridges and Barriers to Successful Integration.

Washington, DC: The Urban Institute. Retrieved from http://webarchive.urban.org/ UploadedPDF/410802_Religion.pdf

Mears, D. P., Roman, C. G., Wolff, A., & Buck, J. (2006). Faith-Based Efforts to Improve Prisoner Reentry: Assessing the Logic and Evidence. *Journal of Criminal Justice, 34,* 351-367.

New Zealand Catholic Bishops Conference. (1999). Creating New Hearts: Moving from Retributive to Restorative Justice. In H. Bowen & J. Consedine, eds., *Restorative Justice: Contemporary Themes and Practice.* Lyttelton, NZ: Ploughshares Publications.

Nolan, P. (2004). *When Prisoners Return: Why we Should Care and how you and your Church Can Help.* Maitland, FL: Xulon Press.

Office of Juvenile Justice and Delinquency Prevention (2012). Disproportionate Minority Contact: OJJDP in Focus. Retrieved from https://www.ojjdp.gov/pubs/239457.pdf

Petersen, R. L. (2002). Reconciliation and Forgiveness in Christian Theology: A Public Role for the Church in Civil Society. Retrieved from http://www.goarch.org/ special/pluralistic2002/presentations/petersen

Petersilia, J. (2003). *When Prisoners Come Home: Parole and Prisoner Reentry.* New York: Oxford University Press.

Pew Forum on Religion and Public Life. (2009). *Faith-Based Programs Still Popular, Less Visible.* Washington, DC: Pew Research Center.

Pew Research Center. (2012). *Religion in Prisons: A 50-State Survey of Prison Chaplains.* Washington, DC: Pew Research Center Forum on Religion and Public Life.

Pew Trust (2016). National Imprisonment and Crime Rates Continue to Fall. Retrieved from http://www.pewtrusts.org/~/media/assets/2017/03/pspp_national_ imprisonment_and_crime_rates_fall.pdf

Pounder, S. (2008). Prison Theology: A Theology of Liberation, Hope, and Justice. *Dialogue: A Journal of Theology, 47* (3), 278-291.

Prison Fellowship. (2018). Organizational website. Retrieved April 22, 2018, from https://www.prisonfellowship.org/about/justicereform/

Roberts, M. R., & Stacer, M. J. (2016). In Their Own Words: Offenders' Perspectives on   Their Participation in a Faith-Based Diversion and Reentry Program. *Journal of Offender Rehabilitation, 55,* 466-483.

Ruth, H. & Reitz, K. (2006). *The Challenge of Crime: Rethinking Our Response.* Cambridge, MA: Harvard University Press.

Schroeder, J. R. (2005). What Does it Mean to be Redeemed? *Beyond Today* (website of United Church of God). Retrieved from https://www.ucg.org/the-goodnews/what-does-itmean-to-be-redeemed

Schroeder, R. D., & Frana, J. F. (2009). Spirituality and Religion, Emotional Coping, and Criminal Desistance: A Qualitative Study of Men Undergoing Change. *Sociological Spectrum, 29,* 718-741.

Schlosser, E. (1998). The Prison-Industrial Complex. *The Atlantic.* Retrieved from https://www.theatlantic.com/magazine/archive/1998/12/the-prisonindustrialcomplex/304669/

Solomon, A., Visher, C., LaVigne, N., & Osborne, J. (2006). *Understanding the challenges of prisoner reentry: Research findings from the Urban Institute's Prisoner Reentry Portfolio.*   Washington, DC: Urban Institute. Retrieved from https://www.urban.org/research/publication/understanding-challenges-prison-erreentry

Stansfield, R., Mowen, T. J., & O'Connor, T. (2017). Religious and Spiritual Support, Reentry, and Risk. *Justice Quarterly, 35* (2), 254-279.

Stephens, R. L. (2015). Mass Incarceration is not the New Jim Crow. Orchestrated Post. Retrieved from http://www.orchestratedpulse.com/2015/04/massincarcerationnot-new-jim-crow/

Strong's Concordance. (2009). Retrieved April 25, 2018, from https://www.blueletterbible.org/lang/lexicon/lexicon.cfm?t=kjv&strongs=h2009.

Travis, J. (2005). *But they all Come Back: Facing the Challenges of Prisoner Reentry.* Washington, DC: Urban Institute Press.

Travis, J., & Visher, C., eds. (2005). *Prisoner Reentry and Crime in America.* Cambridge, UK: Cambridge University Press.

U.S. Department of Justice. (2006). Adults on Probation, in Jail or Prison, and Parole. *Sourcebook of Criminal Justice Online.* Table 6.1. Retrieved from http://www.albany.edu/ sourcebook/pdf/t612006.pdf

United Methodist Church. (2012). *The Book of Disciplines of the United Methodist Church* (12th ed., Vol. 1). Nashville, TN: United Methodist Publishing House.

United Methodist Church. (2015). *Quick UMC Facts*. United Methodist Data Services. Retrieved from http://www.umc.org/gcfa/data-services

United States Sentencing Commission (2016). *Recidivism Among Federal Offenders: A Comprehensive Overview*. Washington, DC: US Sentencing Commission. Retrieved from http://www.ussc.gov/sites/default/files/pdf/research-and-publications/researchpublications/2016/recidivism_overview.pdf

Urban Ministry (n.d.). Best Practices Checklist: Ex-Offender Reentry Programs. Retrieved from http://www.urbanministry.org/wiki/best-practices-checklistexoffender-reentry-programs

Wacquant, L. (2009). *Punishing the Poor: The Neoliberal Governance of Insecurity*. London: Polity.

Wagner, P., & Rabuy, B. (2017). Mass Incarceration: The Whole Pie 2017. Retrieved from https://www.prisonpolicy.org/reports/pie2017.html

Watts, C. M. (n.d.). Christian Ministry in its Theological Context. Retrieved from http://s3.amazonaws.com/tgc-documents/journal-issues/6.3_Watts.pdf

Western, B. (2006). *Punishment and Inequality in America*. New York: Russell Sage Foundation.

Western, B., & Wildeman, C. (2009). The Black Family and Mass Incarceration. *The Annals of the American Academy, 621*, 221-242.

Zimring, F. & Hawkins, G. (1991). *The Scale of Imprisonment*. Chicago: University of Chicago Press.

Curriculum Vitae

- Superior writing, communication, organizational, event planning, recruitment, admissions, development, fundraising, and project management skills
- Exceptional interpersonal and relationship-building skills; demonstrated excellence in partnering with students, faculty, staff, senior leadership, and internal/external stakeholders
- Demonstrated success in serving as a trusted source of information, point-of-contact for diverse constituencies, and cultivating a positive workplace environment with camaraderie, humor, and demonstrated excellence.

Education

- DMin., Andover Newton Theological School @ Yale, Candidate, 2018
- S.T.M., Yale University Divinity School
- M.Div., Yale University Divinity School
- M.A.S.S., Florida A &M University (double concentration political science/public administration)
- B.A., Florida A&M University Honors Program, magna cum laude, exemplary scholar, Political Science/Prelaw,
- Experience abroad: Paris, France, El Salvador, Costa Rica

Professional Licenses

- Ordained Clergy, National Baptist USA, INC
- Licensed Clergy, National Baptist USA, INC
- Notary Public, State of CT

Experience

Assistant Director of Admissions & Recruitment –
Yale University Divinity School (2015-Present)

- Evaluate all admission applications, interview prospective applicants, and independently assess each application against a variety of factors, including the applicant's strength, weaknesses and potential contribution to the Yale Community
- Analyze and independently assess overall records to determine if applicants are appropriate for admissions committee review
- Develop public presentations designed to promote Yale to prospective applicants.
- Manage admissions efforts as they relate to particular substantive areas such as diversity, communications, recruiting, operations, and technology. Provides strategic vision as it relates to this area.
- Expanding and advancing the awareness, recognition, and reputation of YDS.
- Identifying and recruiting the most qualified prospective students to optimize the number, quality and diversity of applications
- Improving YDS student selectivity through the use of meticulous admission standards of selection using counseling and marketing initiatives
- Maximizing the enrollment yield of incoming YDS students who are of the highest quality possible
- Maintain the maintenance of all online files and applications through technoloutions; a highly sophisticated application database
- Proficient in Word, Excel, PowerPoint, and Outlook scheduling. Experienced in Yale systems; e.g., Technolutions
- Schedule meetings and coordinate travel for multiple calendars
- Oversee and train student workers on Yale Divinity School Admissions, policies, procedures, and projects

Admissions Assistant – Yale University Divinity School (2012-2015)

- Represented the Admissions Office in a positive manner as the first point of contact for prospective students and visitors

Dr. Herron Keyon Gaston

- Conducted campus tours to familiarize students with YDS and the larger University Community
- Assisted with the development of enrollment marketing publications and communications including letters, brochures, website posting, electronic mail and other mediums
- Took part in recruitment and enrollment activities such as "open house" to help recruit prospective students
- Traveled to colleges and universities within the United States with admissions personnel to identify and recruit top performing students
- Assisted in creating and maintaining all student files
- Monitored all files consistently to ensure required and updated documentation

Executive Administrative Assistant of Admissions & Recruitment –
Graduate Studies & Research, Florida A & M University (2009-2010)
- Represented the college in a positive manner by acting as first point of contact
- Promoted the college through college fairs and social networking activities
- Communicated with the undergraduate college to identify high performing students – Reviewed students' applications for eligibility
- Provided students with information on admission procedures
- Provided a strategic vision to optimize recruitment efforts
- Assisted students with filling out admissions forms
- Conducted campus tours to familiarize students with the campus
- Represented the graduate college on career fairs and student events
- Answered questions regarding academic programs
- Provided information regarding the college's courses and financial aid eligibility
- Managed and maintained the university wide database
- Assisted students in applying for financial aid
- Traveled to colleges and universities throughout the United States and Brazil
- Assisted in the interview process of prospective students via skype, oovoo, googlehangout, and the use of other online technologies

Senior Pastor/ Chief Financial Officer, Summerfield United Methodist Church, Bridgeport, CT (2015 – Present)

- Oversee payroll, budgets, and requisitions for all senior level church staff
- Oversee all boards and auxiliaries pertaining to all after school programs
- Supervise childport daycare center in conjunction with Bridgeport Hospital
- Serve as the chief officer over all meetings pertaining to church affairs
- Recruit, train and support all volunteer staff and young adults
- Plan and oversee the development of weekly congregational worship
- Chair of Bridgeport Revitalization Committee that meets regularly at the church
- Teach bible study, preach, and lead prayer meetings weekly

Teaching Assistant, Gateway Community College, New Haven, CT (2014 – 2016)

- Assisted faculty with classroom instruction, exams, record keeping, and other miscellaneous projects
- Obtained materials needed for classes, including texts and other materials
- Corresponded with students using educational tools such as Blackboard and other campus communication systems
- Created materials such as a syllabus, visual aids, answer keys, supplementary notes, and course websites

Senior Educational/ Criminal Justice Consultant/ Program Manager, Gaston Justice Coalition, LLC (2013 – Present)

- Provide communities with a strategic vision, programmatic structure, and foster financial resources necessary to save at-risk inner city youth and young adults from crises such as gun violence, drugs, youth illiteracy, and chronic unemployment
- Advise law enforcement and provided them with diversity training for engaging minority communities

- Provide educational leadership training, assist underrepresented minorities find jobs, and assist in vocational development

Associate Director, Health Promotion Program Initiatives, Inc. (2012 – 2013)
- Coordinated and administered assigned County health promotion programs
- Assessed, planned, and administered public health programs
- Managed a staff of four employees and ten volunteers
- Recruited, trained, and supervised program volunteers
- Developed drafts, newsletters, media releases, social media postings, policies, presentations, and program materials
- Provided community health improvement assistance, consultations, and guidance to community groups

Legislative Analyst, Florida Department of Correction, Executive Office of the Governor, Tallahassee, FL
- Proposed solutions for reentry in targeting individuals with mental health issues
- Defined procedures to develop comprehensive and individualized service plans based on results of assessments and evaluations
- Assisting in building consensus between communities and local law enforcement agencies to assist in reentry programs
- Advised the Florida Council on the Social Status of Black Men and Boys by implementing preventative measures in the corrections system
- Advised inmates regarding policies and procedures to obtain a Florida identification, social security card, and driver's license prior to release

CPSIA information can be obtained
at www.ICGtesting.com
Printed in the USA
LVHW051352070419
613260LV00017B/571/P

9 781480 983649